HURT PEOPLE HIGHWAY

BY: NOREEN MCCLENDON

2
Hurt People Highway

HURT PEOPLE HIGHWAY

BY: NOREEN MCCLENDON

NOAH'S ARK PUBLISHING

HURT PEOPLE HIGHWAY

© September 2018 by *NOREEN MCCLENDON.*

ISBN 978-0692-18176-8

Noah's Ark Publishing
Service 8549 Wilshire Blvd.,
Suite 1442
Beverly Hills, CA 90211
www.LAVALDREAMS.com
noahsarkpublishing@gmail.com
Lavaldreams / Noah's Ark Publishing Service LLC

Formatted by Jenine May, President Kingdom Scribes

Edited by Brady Rhoades

TABLE OF CONTENTS

Dedication

"This book is dedicated to Yahweh, who directed every word and everyone that has ever experienced hurt in a relationship. It is further dedicated to the many people that have taught me about relationships along the way including the men of the Francisco Homes and the women of the California Institution for Women. Most of all, it is dedicated to my family that I love so much."

INTRODUCTION

How did I get here? Oh, that's right. It was the road travelled so often by so many before. The road from confident, strong, beautiful black man behind the walls through the gates of panic, self-doubt, fear, insecurity to full-blown identity crisis. I took that ride with you down that dark road. I should have asked the conductor to stop somewhere along the way and got off, but I kept holding on to the poles of stabilization that were your letters, cards and promises. I know he's in there. You look the same, you talk the same, you even laugh the same -- whenever I get to hear it. But it's all a mirage because you don't know who the hell you are. But I love you still. My love, the currency of exchange, the price of admission to that crowded highway of hurt people that leads to hurt people. . .

The excerpt above is from the poem, *Hurt People Highway*, that I wrote in 2013 to capture the pain I was feeling at the end of a failed relationship. I was encouraged by a friend, Melinda Williams, to write my pain. She told me that God told her to tell me to write my pain and that one day I would help a lot of people with my pain.

I had never written a piece of spoken word before. But I try to be obedient to dictates that come from GOD. Come on. I also have a penchant for helping people. Nothing beats a failure but a try and I was certainly willing to try. I had to. I recognized that there were so many relationships in which the man had been incarcerated and when he was released, the relationship failed.

Just as with many other people, prior to my own experience, I believed that the relationships

7

failed because the man had been stringing the woman along for the sake of getting her to put money on his books, send packages and provide general support while incarcerated and now that he was home he no longer needed her and could move on. This does happen, but it is not always the case and, more often than not, has nothing to do with why the relationship fails post incarceration.

I know in my relationship, the man couldn't possibly have been using me for finance because the things I did for him financially while he was incarcerated, he never asked me to do. I asked him how I could do those things. It was not until just prior to his release that he asked me for financial assistance. It was a very small amount and I was super happy to do it. So I know that if the plan was to use me financially, he certainly was a failure at that because he wouldn't ask for help.

However, I discovered something else that I had never heard anyone speak about before. It was the identity crisis that men (I have since learned that women experience the same identity crisis post incarceration) face when they are released. It causes them stress, confusion and fear that renders them unwilling to focus on a relationship right out of prison. They are overwhelmed with reintegrating back into society. They often feel less than a man and shame at not having a way to provide so they leave the relationship. Families have broken up because of this. It is a devastating side effect of the United States' addiction to mass incarceration.

After I wrote the piece, I didn't exactly know what to do with it. Melinda didn't tell me that part. I was informed about a fundraiser for a halfway house through community work that I do. They were going to have spoken word, music and speakers at a coffee house to raise money for the halfway house. I figured, ok, this is probably a good audience to present this piece. They certainly will understand what I'm talking about.

So, I go to the fundraiser, sign up to present, sit through several presentations, and then it's my turn. I get up and begin. About 20 to 30 seconds in, the room is silent. The people ordering coffee are quiet. There are no side conversations. Every eye in the place is on me.

When I'm done, the room roars with applause. People come up to me and tell me how much they enjoyed it. Several men tell me that they have never heard anybody talk about the experience in that way. A nun affiliated with the halfway house, who is about 80 years old, asks me if she can have a copy of the poem. I hand her my folded copy, grateful that she thought enough of the poem to want a copy.

Afterward, my business mind kicked in and I realized that I didn't have it copyrighted. Bad move, I thought. I promised to get copies of the poem for some of the men from the halfway house. A couple months later I received a call from the halfway house program administrator reminding me that a lot of the men were still asking for a copy of the poem. I informed the lady that my copyright was not yet received. I had applied but it had not been received as yet and because of that I was reluctant to simply pass it out to a lot of people. Further, I wasn't interested in it just being handed out to the men. If they wanted to have a conversation about what I wrote, I was willing to do that, but I didn't just want to give it to people to read with no context. This led to me facilitating a weekly self-help group on relationships at a halfway house of men who were formerly serving life sentences.

In the five-plus years of weekly sessions, I have learned so much about relationships. In order to keep the sessions interesting for the men, I have had to research new topics consistently. We come back to some again and again because they are so important. I learned a lot of valuable things. I believe the Creator taught me these things to "help a lot of people," just as Melinda told me. This book is a compilation of the lessons I learned through my own experiences with failed relationships and the ones He gave me to share at the halfway house and in the women's prison, where I teach a weekly self-help group on life skills.

There have been a few principles that are consistent in so many failed relationships. These are the toll roads and the price of admission to the Hurt People Highway. I hope this book can prevent someone from setting themselves up for pain and, in the most extreme cases, entering Heartbreak Hotel. I hope readers walk away with a few tools under their belts to prevent them from engaging in behavior at the beginning of relationships that is almost certain to lead to pain. I will tell you now, *it is all in the selection process!* Select wisely and you give yourself the best chance there is to have a good, healthy relationship.

Although my relationship with the incarcerated man came to an end, I am so grateful for the experience. I experienced a kind of love that I had never had before - a love free of fear. It was a blessing and if I can help others through that experience of pain and hurt, then it was all worth it.

Chapter 1

DADDY'S HURT

- *Who am I*

Throughout my lifetime, I have learned a lot about relationships. The one thing that remains true of every person I know, and lots of people I don't know, is that the early lives of people influence their entire lives. This is true in healthy and unhealthy ways. For me, I had to look deep into myself to identify the elements of my childhood that affected my relationships. Most particularly, my relationships with men.

I grew up the youngest of six children. Three were my parents' biological children and three were my cousins who my mother took in after my father and their parents became hooked on heroin in the 1960's.

I was the baby of the family and treated very well. We grew up in the Champlost Homes projects in Philadelphia, Pennsylvania. I am a very proud, self-described project baby. I was well fed and well educated because my mother insisted on sending us to school out of the neighborhood, and I was well loved and very well protected by the entire neighborhood.

- *The relationship with my Daddy*

My parents were married but separated very early in my life. They would not officially divorce until my teenaged years. My father lived within walking distance of my house, so I saw him fairly regularly. When I visited him, he treated me like a princess. He made my favorite breakfast and cut up my steak at dinner. He literally carried me around until I was almost 12 years old.

One of my favorite things was that he would walk me around the house with my feet on his shoes holding my hands. He even let me have a sip of his beer while he taught me to reload bullets and how to shoot rifles and pistols. He would take us to Bucks County, Pennsylvania to a shooting range and we would shoot targets. He was an avid hunter and I loved the game he caught. I would watch him clean it. I never forgot when he shot a big deer buck. We ate good from that hunting trip because he shot a couple rabbits too.

On the trips to the rifle range, he would stop and buy me a Yahoo Chocolate Milk. It was my favorite. He would take us on the subway to his job cleaning courtrooms. He allowed me to sit in the judge's seat, which seemed enormous as a little girl. My Daddy had a bookstand in the bathroom, a habit that he passed on to his sons and daughter.

While my brothers actually had some form of table or stand to hold books in their bathrooms, I read in the bathroom regularly. I became an avid reader because the behavior was encouraged by my Daddy. But my earliest memory of my father is one of him in a drug rehabilitation facility. My grandparents put their three sharply dressed grandchildren in the car and took us on, what seemed to me to be, a long ride to a place that had rolling hills. In the car my Nana told us that our father was sick and that we had to be on our best behavior. I didn't know exactly what that meant, but as I look back, I realize those were words that shaped my relationships with men for decades to come. My Daddy told me often that he loved me, that I was smart, that I was pretty. He complimented me on a lot of things. My Mommy was even more of a champion. So I did not grow up with the traditional low self-esteem. No, I had to have my own brand. Thanks, guys.

- *Loved, adored, treated like a princess, emotionally unavailable*

Because of the life my father led while on drugs and the challenging relationship he had with his mother (which I would only learn the nature and extent of after she passed many years later), my father was what I later termed "emotionally unavailable." He was reluctant to fully open up emotionally. He said the right things and even shared his favorite things with me, but I somehow felt deep inside that the relationship would only continue if I made sure it did.

Daddy's Hurt

One New Year's Eve, when I was about ten or eleven years old, I distinctly remember feeling a sense of urgency to call my Daddy and tell him that I loved him and Happy New Year. I felt that if I didn't, he would not speak to me again. In the conversation, he was very emotional and thanked me profusely for the call. It is strange for a young child to sense that kind of urgency. But something during the call, which I cannot specifically remember today, made me believe then and until this day, that had I not made that call, my father would have discontinued his relationship with me.

Because I was a Daddy's girl, I did everything I could to maintain the relationship with my father. Even as an adult and until his passing in 2013, I took the responsibility to stay in communication, go visit and ensure that we would remain in contact. For example, my father and I did not share the same political views in a lot of areas. I would call him and we would have our regular debate about politics. However, at some point in time, I realized that he was actually angry at me about politics and had not called in months, so I never debated politics with him again.

He was older and I wasn't willing to take the chance that the relationship would end because of things that were neither in his nor my control. I debated him because he told me that I always gave him the best arguments. I was a chip off the old block. My father taught me to think for myself. My mother insisted on it. I was never one to follow the crowd in thinking or action. I was allowed to have my own point of view. I had to express it very respectfully, but I was allowed as a child to have an opinion and a point of view. This was a gift, as I later learned. So many people grow up in families that don't value them as individuals and worse, tell them that a child should be seen and not heard.

I was blessed not to be raised by people that thought this way. But because my father withheld himself emotionally, I always felt that his participation in my life could disappear at any moment. I didn't feel abandoned. I didn't feel unwanted or unloved. I didn't feel neglected. But after many years of studying and researching relationships, I finally found out how my relationship with my father affected my relationships with men. Due to my perception, whether factual or not, that if I didn't do the work, the relationship with my father would end, I always put the needs of the men I dated first. This was true even if it meant that my needs went unmet. That was the unhealthy part.

I also felt deep inside that a man would not stick around unless I gave in on situations that we disagreed on, even if my feelings were hurt. It was hard to see this for years because it was counter-balanced by my mother's influence, which taught me not to take crap off of anybody. How was I to reconcile the two? It took years to solve the puzzle.

• *What Nana taught me with a single sentence*

The answer to my puzzle was that trip to the drug rehabilitation facility to see my father and the words of my Nana. "Your father is sick and you guys needs to be on your best behavior." When we arrived, he was able to talk, he wasn't confined to a bed. He

17

Daddy's Hurt

walked me on his shoes, just like he always did. He hugged and kissed me. He allowed us to roll down the grassy hills. He talked with my grandparents. He seemed fine to me. BUT, he was sick and I had to be on my best behavior.

As a very young child, I must have processed that situation in a way that said even though he is quite capable of everyday function, he is sick and I have to be compassionate about his feelings, needs and circumstances. This created a dynamic in our relationship that I was always responsible for maintaining the relationship and ensuring that I did not upset or hurt him because he was sick and later, because he had been hurt during the drug and rehab processes.

I recall him telling a story, just once, about how everyone takes advantage of a drug addict, including the police. He talked about having to bathe in the sink of a gas station and how humiliating it was but that it was more important to be clean. Strange things came up about his life that further cemented the idea that he had been hurt and was sick. Therefore, as the "well, strong one," it was up to me to sacrifice what I wanted, and worse, what I needed, for the good of the relationship.

This empathy and concern didn't stop at my Daddy. It extended to the plight of all Black men. I remember fighting the school bully because he was picking on a little boy from Africa who was new to the school. The injustices inflicted upon men in my community always affected me deeply. The injustice still affects me deeply. It may be how I wound up engaged in gang intervention, prison work, managing little league football teams for 15 years and hanging out at the fraternity house in college. I have been drawn to men and their well-being. I am, for better or worse, most comfortable in a room full of men. Always have been. It surely had something to do with the fact that by the time I was of an age to really remember a lot of detail, my brothers were running the house. My cousin/sisters were grown and out of the house so our house was the "hang-out" for the neighborhood boys. I think my sensibilities are more masculine than feminine, despite the fact that I am a girly girl. I love make-up and dress up. I don't like my hands dirty. But I am so at home on a construction site full of men. I have been interested in men and helping them my entire life. Now I have learned that in order for me to have a healthy relationship, I have to require help *from* men. Men need to be needed.

This thinking in a relationship with my father was unhealthy and inappropriate according to divine, universal order, but it was much worse in relationships with men. It set me up for a lot of hurt and being taken advantage of. If you don't make your needs known, people will overlook them every time. I have learned that any time I put someone's needs before my own, I am making an idol of them and it must fall, by divine order. In that my body is the temple of the Most High, if I revere someone above me, then I am engaging in idol worship and demanding that the relationship be taken down.

So ultimately, what I learned from my Nana's words and the experiences with my Daddy, who I called Daddy until his death in 2013, is that I should have compassion and empathy for the trials and tribulations of men. I should make my needs secondary to those things. When the man is not available to meet my emotional needs, just bear it. Be easy to get along with. Be accommodating. Be sweet. Be encouraging. Be loving. ALL of those traits are great traits in a woman. Make no mistake about that. It is probably why 100% of all the men that have ever spent any real time with me always come back to confess that they should have stayed with me. I have a long list of men that love me to this day, even though we are not together.

However, the challenge comes when, according to the definition of healthy, there is no balance. When the wonderful woman is not receiving the same empathy and compassion. When her emotional and/or physical needs are not being met. Let me digress here for a second. Women need and want sex too. Sometimes it is the man that doesn't want to have sex enough. It is not always the woman. When I experienced this for the first time, it was an eye-opener. I had never had that experience before. In my experience, even if the man didn't want to be in a relationship with me, he always wanted more sex with me. It was confusing and hurtful. But by the time I experienced this, thankfully, I knew it wasn't ME. It did not affect my self-esteem.

I later learned that it was because the man had been masturbating in the shower, a habit he developed while incarcerated, and he would not get an erection when he was ready to have sex with me. He finally stopped masturbating and the sex was fine. I have also learned that this was not just this man or the only reason men avoid sex with their partners. I

Daddy's Hurt

know of a couple that was married a very long time and would go years, literally years, without sex. It was not the woman who did not want the sex. It was the man. So don't believe the stereotype that men can't live without sex and women are the ones that withhold sex in a relationship.

I will say this: The key to correcting any problem in a relationship is to acknowledge that it exists and communicate about the matter. Avoiding the conversation only leaves room for imagination. The last thing you need in a problem-relationship is the imagination running wild. It is even more important, but less likely to happen, when the problem is sexual in nature to communicate about a problem. It is an area where people tend to assume that there is someone else involved when the other party doesn't want to have sex. This creates unnecessary challenges in the relationship.

For any man reading this, talk to your partner about sexual dysfunction. It is an important part of the relationship for her as well as for you. I spoke to a woman whose boyfriend came home from prison with erectile dysfunction and they never, ever talked about it and it ultimately ruined their relationship. She knew of another couple that was married and the same thing happened when the husband came home from prison. It dissolved their family.

I strongly believe it could have been avoided if they had discussed the sexual issues. In fact, I interviewed a very courageous man who came home from prison and suffered erectile dysfunction when he came home. He was able to explain what he experienced, what he believes caused the dysfunction and how he overcame it. We will call him Mr. Courageous for the sake of his privacy, but also because it took great courage for him to be so honest and provide so much detail about his experience in an effort and willingness to help someone else.

His assessment is in line with the pieces of information I was able to gather from conversations with other men who had served time. Mr. Courageous went into depth about the problem and solidified for me that there are two common factors that contribute to erectile dysfunction in men upon release from prison. When we spoke, he talked about both issues.

One issue is that in order to survive the prison environment, it is critical to turn off sexual drive at some level. Men have to turn off the emotions that produce sexual desire. If they are not homosexual and not willing to engage in homosexual activity for the sake of sexual release, they have to turn off those emotions. Not to mention that emotions in prison can be very dangerous for lots of reasons that I won't explore here. But anyone who has served time in prison will understand. Once anyone has turned off desire, it is not that easy to simply turn it on again. It requires conditioning to turn off a very basic, human, natural, healthy desire.

Like most things in prison, it is about programming. To program the brain not to want sex regularly for a healthy adult male takes effort and time. Upon release, the programming has to be undone, but it takes time as well. Mr. Courageous explained to me that some men never get over it. He was given Viagra, but it didn't work. That was

22
Daddy's Hurt

frightening. He was given Cialis and it would give him an erection, but as soon as there was physical contact, even touch as elementary as putting on a condom might cause him to reach an orgasm. It was very challenging. He identified his reality, which supported what another person shared with me on the subject. There has to be an emotional attachment or their body simply will not respond. It requires them to develop genuine feelings for the woman before they can be sexual with her. Even if she is physically attractive to them and willing, if they do not feel emotionally attached to her, they will not be able to perform.

As I shared with Mr. Courageous, in an odd way, it is a blessing that they need to be emotionally attached to have sex. Today, people engage in sex too casually. I will discuss this in more detail later, but for now, just follow me. Our society suffers greatly due to people engaging in casual sex in many ways: sexually transmitted diseases are real; unplanned pregnancies leading to children being born of parents that don't even know each other and are often incompatible, bitter and angry at the reality that they are now going to have a child they didn't plan to have; children being raised in single-parent households; people hurting each other because they were hurt when they wanted more from the casual sexual relationship and did not get it; the men and women that resort to physical violence because of the pain they feel being confronted with the reality of their choice or seeing their sexual partner with one of their other sexual partners.

These scenarios are played out daily on talk shows and reality television. With that knowledge, I explained to Mr. Courageous that it is a blessing for him and society as a whole if men coming home can't perform sexually with women they are not emotionally attached to. While it may be a challenge for the male-ego, it is good for society. It will not likely produce offspring to parents that don't know each other, much less *like and respect* each other. There is a better likelihood that if they are not able to remain a couple, they will be reasonable toward each other in making healthy co-parenting decisions. This will reduce the number of children who must navigate the jungle of dysfunctional parents. After all, it is hard "raising parents," much less dysfunctional, unhealthy parents. Less hurt, dysfunctional children means less hurt, dysfunctional adults sent out into the world to wreak havoc. Less dysfunctional adults produces fewer dysfunctional families, neighborhoods, communities and society. So the inability to perform sexually with a woman they don't know is good for society.

The second factor is masturbation. This is true for men who served time in prison and men who have not. Mr. Courageous explained to me that masturbation in prison is not just a sexual action. It is also used to relieve stress. The prison universe has so many stress-producing elements that inmates often masturbate just to relieve the stress. This constant practice programs the penis to the pressure from the hand, which can be tightened or released at just the right time to reach orgasm. The vagina, no matter how tight, can't compete with the strength of a man's hands, just as a man's hands or tongue can't exert the same pressure on a clitoris as a sex toy.

So, while masturbation may be a great short-term solution to stress relief and sexual need, it is detrimental to the body's natural process. Once the body becomes used to artificial means of stimulation, it begins to require it. This becomes a challenge trying to return to normal sexual relations. Another man who had never been incarcerated explained that he, too, had a problem reaching an orgasm in a vagina because no vagina could exert as much pressure as his hand and he masturbated chronically. In order to correct this problem, people have to stop masturbating for a period of time.

One way that the men I know of who have had this problem handle it is to simply avoid becoming sexual with a woman. In my case, the man was very affectionate with me. This made it even more confusing. Initially, he would not discuss the erectile dysfunction with me. This went on for months. One night when he was finally ready to have sex and could not get an erection in the moment, it opened the door for a conversation. After that night and discussion, we were able to resolve the issue. The point is that once the conversation is held, the issue can be resolved.

In the case of the woman whose significant other returned from prison and would not discuss the problem with her, her initial thought was that there was another woman involved. Then she began to believe that he was not attracted to her personally. Then he became angry about it and began to take it out on her. This destroyed the relationship. Many years after the relationship ended, he confessed to her what the real problem was. Like me, she was shocked to learn that that was the problem. She was hurt that he did not trust her enough to talk to her about it when it was happening. She was sad that he suffered alone. She would have encouraged him to see a doctor to find out if there was a health condition causing it or something else. The really sad part is that he could have satisfied her in so many other ways and because she loved him, she would have stayed and the relationship did not have to end.

Avoiding sex with the woman they are in a relationship with leaves her to imagine why he won't have sex with her. In my case, he wanted to kiss me, hold me, feel on me but not have sex. Mr. Courageous told me a story of a woman that he was very physically attracted to and she was making it really clear that she wanted him sexually. He even made out with her. He did not know her well and knew that his body would not be able to perform so he ended the foreplay immediately. He never discussed anything with her. My previously incarcerated man would do the same thing early in our relationship and I didn't understand why. Now I understand. The fair, but extremely hard thing for a man to do, is to talk to her about it or wait until he is emotionally attached to her. For those who don't know what this is like, try putting yourself in the man's shoes. Then try to think about the confusion the woman experiences. This is a huge problem that can be addressed through effective communication.

I understand that a man coming home from prison, who has nothing to offer his woman from a financial standpoint (does not know who he is, what he does and how much he makes, in the words of Steve Harvey in his best-selling book *Act Like a Lady, Think Like a Man*), will not want to commit or remain committed to her. If he can't perform sexually on top of not being able to provide for her, it destroys his self-esteem and he feels useless to his woman.

Men need to be needed. If a man feels that he can't meet *any* of his woman's needs, he is likely to walk away from the relationship. The feeling of inadequacy in men is also why men tend to *cheat down*. That means that they cheat with a person who has less to offer than the person they are with. The reason for this is simple: The person makes them feel like a man and the woman who they are with makes them feel less like a man. This often can be the result of the man's circumstances, but can also be produced when the woman is constantly pointing out her man's faults or trying to polish him up and make him better -- in her eyes.

After speaking to a candid woman, my own experience, speaking to a man who was part of a support group of about seven men who grew up together, but all had served at least twenty years in prison, another man who had served more than twenty-seven years and Mr. Courageous, I have come to the conclusion that there is a real sexual challenge that is created when men are incarcerated for a long period of time. Their minds have to be altered to survive the environment they are in. Physically, while the penis does still achieve an erection, the body may become programmed to only do so when they are alone because there was no other person there when they achieved an erection for years.

Because no actual person was there, they were only able to achieve an erection by visualizing a previous experience with a person they truly loved and now their mind can only achieve and maintain an erection in similar circumstances. This side effect of incarceration has to become an open discussion. Not only are the men fighting the physical and mental challenges in silence and the women are confused and hurt by the mixed signals sent by the men, everyone is fighting the myth that when a man comes home, he is going to want to "fuck like a rabbit."

The myth causes women to expect regular sex when he comes home. When it doesn't happen, she is confused. He is suffering in silence and allowing the confusion to persist because he may not fully understand why his penis is erect when he wakes up in the morning, he loves and is attracted to the woman in his life, was always able to become erect thinking about her when he was incarcerated but can't physically reach an erection or maintain one when he is in her presence.

In fact, a lot of women pursue a man who is fresh out of the penitentiary because of the myth. They want to be the first person he has sex with. The additional pressure on him is real and unfair. However, the only way to correct the problem is to acknowledge that it exists, face and address it, and destroy the myth. Thank you for following me as I digressed to address something that is pervasive but still secret. I hope someone receives understanding and healing.

Daddy's Hurt

There were things that I did not learn about relationships because my parents weren't together. My grandparents on my father's side were together. My grandfather worked two jobs as long as I can remember. When I went to Nana and Pop Pop's house, I watched my grandmother care for my grandfather in very specific ways. She cooked, she cleaned and we always had to take him to work or pick him up from work. There was the occasional pinochle party in the basement with friends. There were vacations. I believed that they loved each other. My grandmother made it a point to tell me that all men were not bad. At the time, I was young, but I perceived that she was trying to counter-balance what she *thought* my mother was teaching me at home. She *thought* my mother was bashing my father and men to me.

My mother was raised, primarily, by her aunts. Her mother died when she was three years old. Her father left her with her grandparents but her aunts did a lot of the work raising her. None of them had husbands while I was alive. The truth is that my mother was very clear that I had to depend on myself, not a man or anyone else. I was going to have to work to have what I wanted. I should never let a man beat me. She did not have a series of men in and out of our home. There was one "uncle" that I later found out was actually her boyfriend, but he only came to the house to be with her when we were asleep, unless he was there to attend to something that needed to be fixed or built.

It would be years before my sibling would tell me that he was her boyfriend. It would also be years, not until my teenaged years, that my mother openly had a boyfriend in my presence. So I think my grandmother thought my mother was giving anti-man speeches to me on a regular basis and she needed to point out that all men were not bad.

My mother never bad-mouthed my father to me when I was young. As I got older she would tell me the truth of a situation involving him. She told me that he had beat her up the night before when she could not hide the black eye he gave her because she did not want to be with him. She did not say he was worthless or no good and she certainly never taught me that all men were bad. In fact, I would later learn that my mother would slip my father money so that he could take us out for the day. He would buy us hoagies from Blimpie's with money she gave him. She did this because she knew that we needed to spend time with our father. She did not want to be with him, but she knew we needed it and she helped to facilitate it until he was back on his feet and able to do it for himself.

My father did, thankfully, get firmly on his feet after his drug addiction. He got his college degree and before he retired was the director of four mental health facilities in the City of Philadelphia. My father was an extraordinary man of intelligence, wit and humor. When my Nana told me that all men weren't bad, I simply told her that I knew that. That was the end of the conversation and the education about men from her.

What I didn't learn was when and how to assert my needs or the importance of *requiring something* from a man. Think about it this way. If a man needs to be needed and you do not place any requirements on spending time with you, what kind of challenge is that? Men are hunters and gatherers by nature. They love the chase. If you don't create anything for them to chase, they lose interest.

There is a saying that men love bitches. I am not sure if they love the bitchy part as much as meeting the high demands. They feel accomplished. Be careful though. My old boss told me that his wife was high maintenance, but it was a challenge and he loved being able to meet the challenge. However, when she was not sweet and kind, he left.

So, I offer that you can set really high standards, but you have to be nice to be around. Nobody wants to be around a person with a bad attitude, I don't care how cute she is or how much of a challenge she presents. I didn't know when to put my needs first, what I could and should expect a man to do in a relationship. Other than work and provide, which I figured out from my grandparents and other influences in my life, I had no idea what a man was expected to do for me. I didn't know what I could and should expect. The problem with that is, having no expectations produces nothing. I became a place to "get" without actually having to "give."

Giving is part of the getting cycle. It is a crucial part of the cycle. It is fine for one person to give most of the time if that is their personality and character. However, at some point, that person must receive in order to keep the cycle going.

• *The consequences of my incomplete knowledge*

Having an incomplete knowledge of what a relationship should be caused me to settle for pieces. Settling for pieces caused me hurt and pain. There was lots of disappointment.

In my twenties, I experienced the most painful relationship I have ever had. It taught me a lot about what I did not want and how subtly bad relationship habits can exist and be allowed to form at the beginning of the relationship. It taught me a lot of things about asserting my needs, wants and desires. It also taught me that unless I consent to bad treatment by participating, it won't happen in my relationship more than once. My mother had a saying (in fact, she had a saying for almost everything): "They can't ride your back if you're not bent over."

It makes a lot of sense and is so true. If I allow someone to monopolize my time and admit that they have no commitment or responsibility toward me, I have bent over and made my back available for the ride. I didn't have an example to look at so I focused heavily on being ready for a relationship. What I never asked myself was if the man was qualified to be with me. It was not so much qualification in terms of what society tells we should be looking for. Society tells women that we should have a handsome man making lots of money, and that he is romantic and always there for his children.

Those are not the qualifications that I realized I needed. I need a man that knows himself so well because he has a personal relationship with his Creator. He needs to have this relationship so that he

Daddy's Hurt

can use it as a guide for how to treat me -- like the Creator treated his bride. I have found, however, that the closer the relationship a man has to his Creator, the better his finances and looks tend to be. It's a side-effect. Seriously, when a man has a great relationship with his Creator and uses that as a basis for how he treats his woman and his family, he tends to treat his work life with the same care.

Thus, his finances are better. He can get his hair groomed regularly. He can drive a car that is not subject to break down before he gets to the end of the block. Those things look good on a man. The way you do anything is the way you do everything. If you are responsible when it comes to family and work, you are typically going to have better outcomes for everyone involved in your life. On the other hand, if you are irresponsible with things, the outcome is not very good.

It's just that simple. This is why a good way to determine how a person, man or woman, will treat you is to first look at how they treat themselves. Pay attention to how they take care of their business and pay their bills. How do they respond when they feel sick? Do they go to the doctor or do they always try to tough it out?

If they care more for you than they do for their own health, that is a good sign that there will be difficulty in the relationship. Find out how they treat the people and the job or career they have. If they mishandle those things, all of which are important in a person's life, you should not expect them to treat you with any more care than they treat everything else in their lives. It reminds me of the woman that has a child with a man who already has children that he doesn't support. What in this man's history, that you know of, leads you to believe it's going to be different with you and your child? News flash: It's not! The only way it will be different is if the man makes a change from within that will show up outwardly and it will affect everything, including the relationship and responsibility toward the children he already has. That would be when it might be safe to have children with this person and expect him to be responsible toward them.

- *The foundation for all of the hurt I experienced in relationships*

The foundation for all of the hurt I experienced in relationships was my lack of knowledge of what I deserved. I spent too much time worrying about what my partner needed to be concerned about what I needed. I didn't feel secure in a relationship because I didn't feel secure in the relationship with my father.

Once I learned how a woman was supposed to be treated, from my study of spiritual things in my twenties, I was able to assert my needs, desires and wants. I was no longer willing to settle. I have dated people that most people thought were beneath me since then. However, they were not in my relationship and I know what I need better than anyone else. I realized I deserved and was worthy of being cared for, protected, respected and provided for.

Once that was a reality for me, the type of man that even approached me got much better. For

Daddy's Hurt

everyone reading this: you can only attract what you are. If you are attracting poor quality, look at what you believe about yourself and what you are. That may sting a little bit, but it is the source of all of your outcomes. We are the sum total of our choices. If we choose poor quality, if we are poor quality, we can only expect that we will receive poor quality. This is the law of attraction. It applies whether we want it to or not. It does not discriminate. It shines on the wealthy, poor, old and young.

* *The reason I won't settle for less than what I deserve*

The reason I can no longer settle for less than I deserve is because I believe that I am accepting less for my Creator who inhabits my body and paid a price for it. He died on the cross for me so that I can have Him. If I can have Him, why would I hook him up with a chump? Nah, not me. I only want the best for Him. I am not separate from Him. He lives in me. Since I can't get rid of Him, I have to treat me as royalty. Nobody has to believe what I believe, but it has improved the quality of man that approaches me and most importantly, how that man treats me.

I have ended more relationships with men than men have ended with me. I ended them because they were not providing what I needed. I didn't have all of the language that I am giving you in this book, but I had the behavior. It became important for me to write this book because all of the language became so clear as I was required to do research for my self-help group at a halfway house for men who were formerly serving life sentences. I could not keep this information to myself. It was not given to me for my benefit alone. It was given to me like all information that is divinely-inspired: to share with His people.

• *Where did I get the information to correct my lack of knowledge?*

I was able to overcome my poor relationship habit of always putting the man's needs ahead of my own by looking at the relationship the Creator has with his bride. I turned to the Bible and nature, which is how the Creator provides us proof that He exists and how he operates. I am not here to tell you what to believe or try to get you to believe what I believe. That is not my assignment with this book, nor my intention. However, it would be wrong for me to take credit for information that was *given* to me.

In studying the Bible and other spiritual principles and writings, I learned the importance of order. I talked about order in another chapter. I have read great books that gave me insight into the mistakes I was making. I have watched other couples and, as a result of divine insight, have been able to see the mistakes and positive results based on how couples live the principles that I have been shown.

After learning some very specific principles and applying them to my relationships, I have avoided great hurt, even though the relationships ended. I have never been devastated by a breakup since my twenties. It has been a journey of blessings. I now have a full knowledge of what it takes to have a healthy relationship and am assigned to share that with you in this book.

Chapter 2

HOW DO WE GET HURT?

- *Highway to Heartbreak Hotel*

There is a road that leads to pain. It has signs and wonders that are undeniable. One interesting thing about the Highway to Heartbreak Hotel is that the price of admission is our desire for love and belonging. It can come in the form of a beautiful woman with the most amazing skin and smile you have ever seen. Or the funniest, smartest man you have ever met, who puts your needs first, AT THE BEGINNING.

The problem arises when this is all that the person of interest has and we rush into a sexual relationship without setting ground rules before the true character of the person is revealed. We often ask ourselves how do you know when the person you are interested in is the right one. There is no shortcut to get the answer. The only thing that guarantees it is the right person is to put in the time to get to know them.

Not just what they say, but what they do in a given situation.

One of the tools I have used with success early in a relationship is to listen to the other person's conversation about their interaction with other people that have nothing to do with me. How they deal with other people will be how they will deal with you, any potential children you have, your extended family, your colleagues. If you meet the person and they cheat on the person they are with to be with you, you should pretty well expect that they will cheat on you with someone else. Why? Because the way you do anything is the way you do everything.

People are who they are. Many times early in a relationship, people show the person they are interested in a person who is who they would like to be and want to be perceived to be. It is their representative, their good angel, their image. It is not the totality of the person, just the parts that they want others to see. This is the sales pitch of a used car salesman. In order not to drive that car off the lot onto Hurt People Highway, you have to read the fine print. As the saying goes: The devil is in the details. Yes, the surface may look great, but underneath is where the real person lives. That is the person that you will spend the majority of your time with. No-one is their best self all of the time.

The most interesting thing about the road to pain is that it is a road we travel *at will* and despite the many protestations and danger signs that present along the way urging us to get off, it is our choice to proceed and ultimately, because of our decisions, we suffer on this road. The longer we choose to insist that

How Do We Get Hurt?

this road (relationship) is for us, the more pain we suffer and the more likely that we will check-in to Heartbreak Hotel. But remember, it is our choice and we can prevent checking-in. This is another one of those times I will need a bodyguard to protect me from the darts, daggers and bullets. I need my super power to protect me. No matter. It is the truth.

I had to stop looking at the person who hurt me to learn how and why I got hurt. One of the hardest days of my life was the day that I had to look myself in the mirror in the midst of the most excruciating pain I had ever felt and accept the truth that *it was my fault*. My behavior led to this pain. My willingness to participate in disrespectful, self-sacrificing behavior for the sake of maintaining the relationship was the reason I was in so much pain. Offering my love and even unhappiness to make someone else happy caused me the worst pain I ever felt. It hurt so much because I had violated a major law. I violated universal law by putting someone else's needs before mine. I learned that my body is the temple of the Holy Spirit. It is the "house of the Lord." It is where He inhabits in order to do what He intended to do in this vessel. My body is sacred ground.

Just imagine how wonderfully we would treat ourselves and each other if we accepted that our bodies are sacred ground. Anything I allow to happen to this vessel, in effect, I have allowed to happen to Him. This, mind you, after he made the ultimate sacrifice for ME. Yes, he made it with ME in mind. I repay Him by allowing someone to disrespect it, disregard it, abuse it and wonder why I am in pain. I

How Do We Get Hurt?

don't know people that wake up in the morning and say they want to violate the Creator today. If I met that person, I would run as far away from him or her as possible. This is not the person who simply doesn't believe in a Creator. It is the person who wakes up with the intention to harm the Creator. There is a difference. I want no part of the latter.

For years, I allowed a man I wanted to be in a committed relationships with to have whatever parts of me he wanted with no responsibility to meet my needs. I put his needs and wants before mine. I spent so much time trying to convince him that I was worthy and qualified to be with him. I didn't ask if he was qualified to be with me. I learned that I had given him the power and responsibility to make and keep me happy. The problem with that is, that it is my responsibility. No-one can make me happy. I have to engage in behavior that will meet my needs and the result is more likely to be happiness and/or contentment and if it leads to the ultimate result, there is peace. We all have basic needs. When these needs are met, we feel fulfilled and usually consider ourselves happy and successful. It doesn't matter what other people think of our version of happiness and success. It is our version, our perception that matters. There are a few behaviors that are guaranteed to lead to pain.

- *When someone else's needs go ahead of yours, you have taken that fork in the road and entered the Hurt People Highway*

In the most painful relationship I have ever been in, the needs of the man came first. It started with little disrespectful behaviors that I simply did not realize were disrespectful until hindsight. For example, he worked nights and I worked days. I would allow him to keep me awake talking on the phone well into the early hours of the morning, even though I had to get up for work the next morning. We would have the most engaging and stimulating conversations while he was at work. I enjoyed them. However, I once called him while I was at work during the hours he usually slept and he was quick to scold me and remind me that he worked nights and needed to sleep during the day. I never called him during those hours again. Why was it acceptable for him to keep me awake during the hours that I needed to sleep, but I could not keep him awake during the hours he was supposed to sleep?

It was acceptable because his needs came first. Whatever was necessary to keep him around. This was a man who told me that I was not his girlfriend. If I was not his girlfriend, much less his wife, then what had he deposited in the "Bank of Noreen" that allowed him to make those kind of withdrawals? If his investment in me wasn't large enough to warrant a title, then why was my investment in him so large that I was willing to forego sleep just to talk to him? At some point I had to ask myself this and realize that

How Do We Get Hurt?

he didn't hurt me, I hurt myself by allowing him to invest so little and receive so much.

It is amazing to me that in today's times, women will freely give of their bodies to a man they barely know without so much as a conversation about the nature of the relationship and then wonder why their feelings get hurt. Be clear, it is not only women who do this. Men do the same thing. If I have no right to know what kind of credit you have, what you believe in spiritually, where you live, what kind of relationship you have with your children, your arrest record, any number of things that people deem too personal to ask early in a relationship, then why do you get to have the most sacred part of me?

More importantly, why am I willing to give you access to it? It makes me cringe every time I see it. I cringe because I have done this before. I know beyond any doubt that it is one of those stops along the highway leading to Heartbreak Hotel. Engaging in sexual relations before there is a clear definition of the nature and responsibility of the relationship is a toll booth to the Hurt People Highway. I know of a woman who met a man at work. They began the relationship by making out in the closet at work. There was no conversation about where the relationship was going. They barely knew each other. However, they both put their jobs on the line for the excitement of making out on the job. This led to having sex away from the job. They never discussed what, if anything, the sex meant in the context of their relationship. They never defined the relationship.

After several sexual encounters, the man made his usual call to entice her to come have sex again. She made excuses, all of which he found a solution for. Finally, she said: "I don't think we should see each other any more." He said: "Ok." She was hurt, confused and furious that he simply said ok. She wanted him to fight for the relationship. The problem was that he had no idea why she wanted to end it nor why she was upset. From his standpoint, everything was going fine. He had the benefit of the most sacred part of her, her time and attention, her smile, and whatever else he wanted when he wanted it. She never asked for anything. She never required anything from him. She agreed to participate when he called. He felt everything was going just fine. He had all the benefits of her without any responsibility to her. What a sweet deal. Wouldn't it be great to have the benefits of driving a luxury car without having the responsibility to pay the car note, the maintenance and repair bills or the insurance? I can drive it whenever I want. All I have to do is call and say that I want to drive it today and it is clean, has a full tank of gas, smelling good, comes with a nice cooked hot meal and then I return it when I'm done until I am ready to drive it again. I don't know of anybody who drives that wouldn't sign up for that deal.

Essentially, when we allow people to have access to our time, our intellect, our resources, our talents, our bodies, and Heaven forbid, our finances, without requiring any definition, title or understanding of what it means to have this access, we have devalued our talents and paid a toll to enter that Highway. Usually, this happens because we are auditioning for the part of the other person's soulmate. We meet a person that we believe is what we want. We immediately swing into audition mode. We begin to put our best face on. We show them how talented we are. If we are witty, we share that wit. If we are a good cook, we cook for them. If we have great business knowledge, we give them access to that. If we have resources, we share them. If we think they are cute, we share our bodies.

In a lot of instances, the other person has not even expressed an interest in having access to all of these talents. We simply make them available because we are auditioning to be the next Mr. or Mrs. in their lives. We want them to see what a good catch we are. Did they ask us to be their mate? The slickest trick we play on ourselves is this. In conversation, the other person details what they are looking for in a relationship. It is exactly what we are looking for. We take the huge leap to mean that they want that relationship with us. Well, news flash folks: Unless people say that they want a relationship with you, they don't. If people want a relationship with you, they will come out and declare that very specifically. Why do they do this? Because they don't want any misunderstanding about what is theirs. Once people have decided that they want something to be theirs, they let everyone know it is theirs and, usually, that they don't intend to share it. It is one of the first words little children master: mine, mines even.

- *When you proceed in a relationship without an agreement and definition of what role you are playing and what the nature of the relationship is.*

How Do We Get Hurt?

A mistake I have made in relationships that has caused a lot of pain and confusion is to engage in relationship activities without having any clear understanding of what role I have been given in the other person's life and what the nature of the relationship is. I did this because I did not gather enough information to know the answer. I did not ask the right questions. I did not require any information or particular behavior from the other person. I did not validate the qualifications of the person I was involved with to see if he was qualified to be in a relationship with me.

I have heard people say often that they don't like titles and labels in a relationship. This is a recipe for disaster. If you don't have a title, how do you know what your responsibility to the other person is? You don't. As long as the relationship is undefined, responsibility can be assumed and discarded at will. This saying is great for people who want the benefit of a relationship without the responsibility. It allows them to have access to the other person's talents without being obligated to them.

I allowed a man to monopolize all of my free time, keep me up at night knowing I had to work the next day, have me sexually — only when he wanted to. Late in the relationship, we had a discussion. He remarked that he was always there for me when I needed him. He was. I explained that he was never there when I wanted him to be there. He showed his love by providing for me. I rarely carried a wallet when we were together. If he saw that I needed something at my home, he simply brought it with him the next time he came, no conversation needed.

How Do We Get Hurt?

However, if I wanted him to attend a gathering with my friends or my family, I could not guarantee that he would be there. I had to hold my breath and hope. It was always up to him. Let's face it. Women want their man with them at family and friend functions. I gave this man access to my talents that he chose when he wanted. He especially enjoyed our late night conversations. He told me that nobody ever gave him a better conversation than me. I should have required a commitment for the privilege.

My mistake was to allow him access to the parts of me that he wanted without requiring anything of him. The truth was that I thought he was the absolute best catch I had ever seen. It was true at the time. I just didn't realize that I was the best catch he had ever seen. Because I didn't know what I had a right to expect, the vestiges of my Daddy hurt, I was more concerned that he would walk away and didn't know that I had a right to put a price on access to my time and talents. I didn't want to take the chance that he would walk away if I insisted on having a commitment.

This went on for a few years. One day, after we spent the best time on a four-day vacation where he did anything I wanted to do, he walked into my place of worship with another woman. There were no restrictions on his freedom. He had made no commitment to me. Therefore, he didn't owe me an explanation. I have adopted this saying: If it has no definition it is nothing. This means that if I have no title, I have no position in your life. This doesn't mean that every man I meet has to make a commitment to me in order to spend time with me. What it does

How Do We Get Hurt?

mean is that based on what the man says he wants from me in our relations will depend on how much access to my talents he can have.

I once had a man tell me that he wasn't sure what the nature of our relationship was. He was going through some things and wasn't sure what he was looking for in a relationship at that point in time. That was a signal that I should invest very little of my talents in this situation. I allowed myself to enjoy his time when I felt like it, but only to the level that I felt comfortable that I would not be hurt.

Even more important, I did not assume that we were building a relationship, I did not give him priority over anything else I was doing. If I was on a call when he called, I would call him back. After all, he was not a priority. I did not have sex with him. He was left squarely and clearly in the friend zone. I love my friend. But I don't have sex with my friend. This practice has kept me from acting like a wife while being treated like a casual acquaintance.

- *When we assume what our position is without having a specific conversation and agreement with the person we are in a relationship with.*

People speak in terms that can be interpreted. We read into a statement what we want to hear. If a man says I want to be married and the woman wants to be married, she reads into his statement that they are working toward marriage. She makes this giant leap, "in her favor," because it serves her purposes. It frees her up to act like a wife without the proposal or marriage. She previously set a rule for herself that she will no longer engage in any relationship that is not headed for marriage. When she meets this guy who she thinks fits the bill, he expresses an interest in her and says he wants to be married too, what else does she need to know? She has hit pay dirt -- the happily ever after. Not so fast.

Until they have a clear and specific conversation about their intentions and come to a verbal, mutual agreement about the nature of their relationship, if she gives him access without responsibility, she has violated her own rules. In short, unless they have agreed in very specific terms: I want to build a life with you, I want to date for a while with the intention to see if you are my wife, etc., then she has interpreted the conversation in her favor. She made a leap from what he actually said to what she wanted to hear. This gave her permission to do what she wanted to do anyway. She can now pull out all of her best talents and share them with this man. When the relationship fails to lead to marriage, she is devastated. Why? Because she put her interpretation on what he said.

A simple way to avoid making this mistake is never assume anything. If it is not said and agreed to, it does not exist. If he doesn't tell me he wants to be my man, I don't have a man. I also don't have the responsibility to cook, clean, care for him and his extended family and I certainly don't have the responsibility to have sex with him.

How Do We Get Hurt?

- *Why women stopped asking the question: "Where is this relationship going?"*

The challenge for women in getting to this specific, clearly communicated definition of a relationship is that we have to ask questions to get there. Men have, for as long as I can remember, hated to hear the question: "Where is this relationship going?" Men hear that question and automatically assume that we want to marry you and even worse, control you. Whoa! The scary control monster is here to take away my freedoms.

They start running the other way. So, women stopped asking the question. We are afraid that it will chase you away. In reality, we are enjoying the time spent together, usually beginning to have feelings for you and want to understand what it is that we are engaged in. For me, even more importantly, how should I be behaving at this point? Is it safe for me to allow these feelings to grow? Should I be taking the responsibility to make sure he has dinner every night? Should I offer to take his mother to the doctor to prevent him from having to take off work? Should I do his laundry? Should I expect him to talk to me every day?

All of this should depend on the level of investment each party is making in the relationship. I should only be investing at the level to which the other person is investing in the relationship. I don't want to imply that a relationship is 50/50 or any specific percentage invested. Someone is always going to be giving a little more than the other. In a healthy relationship, that will change at any point in

How Do We Get Hurt?

time. That allows it to balance itself out. It is unhealthy when only one party is always investing more in the relationship. It is out-of-balance and by definition becomes unhealthy.

- *Engaging in sexual relations too early*

There is no mistake that will cause more pain and will almost guarantee hurt than this mistake. There are a couple reasons why this is true. First, it is the most intimate and sacred part of us that we have to offer. Men have a limited ability to engage in sexual relations for purely sexual reasons. Women have virtually no ability, even though many have lied to themselves or truly thought they could, only to meet disastrous results. I say to the men in my groups at the halfway house, there is a string from the vagina to the heart, if you keep tugging on that string, she is going to develop feelings. You don't even have to be the best at the tug either. Maybe there should be a sign at the vagina's entrance that says: **"Warning: Continued tugging will cause emotional attachment for the string's owner or the person tugging."** Maybe it could prevent some truly strong people from getting tangled up in a mess. They would have to be strong because they would be reading the sign at the entrance to the vagina. It's usually hard to resist a tug if you got that close.

Second, once we engage in sex, we lose some of our ability to objectively view the entire person. On the other hand, when we wait to engage in sex, it leaves our objectivity intact and we avoid getting too deep in a relationship before we see the major

How Do We Get Hurt?

character flaws of the person we are interested in. It makes it less tricky to get out of a relationship that has not progressed to a sexual nature.

I know a guy that had a business that he cared deeply about. His business caused him to have to deal with a lot of women. Several women expressed interest in him. He was interested in one woman in particular. He took her to a movie and to one dinner date. They talked on the phone and he saw her when he was in the area she frequented. However, I advised him not to sleep with her until he was sure that he knew her well enough to identify her flaws and until he knew for sure that he wanted a long-term relationship with her.

A few months in, she did something that completely turned him off. He knew instantly that she could never be his long-term mate. He was concerned about how to get out of the relationship. I asked him if he had ever made any commitment to her. He said he had not. I informed him that there was no need to terminate what had never actually began. If they had not defined their relationship then there was no need to get out of it because it didn't exist. Since he had not engaged in sexual behavior with her, she could not say he used her or took advantage of her. He did tell her that he did not want a relationship at this time. Once he told her that, the appropriate response from her, if she wanted to be in a committed relationship, would be to limit the amount of time and talents that she made available to him. She might be unhappy that he was not going to be in a relationship with her, but she could not accuse him of being a bad person or

How Do We Get Hurt?

taking advantage of her and then begin to attack his business.

- *The level of pain and trauma you experience depends on how close you get to Heartbreak Hotel*

On the Highway to Heartbreak Hotel, there are signs along the way warning you that you are in danger and that the danger ahead is worse. We may miss the signs early in the relationship because we are focusing on the wrong things. Depending on what we *want* out of a relationship, we are grading the other person to see if he or she fits.

We often force someone into the mold of what we want in our minds. The signs that they are not what we are looking for or are the exact same thing that has never worked for us in the past, we are focusing on all the reasons "this time will be different."

As soon as we engage in sex, we lose our ability to focus on the small signs. We lose perspective and objectivity. When the little signs of disrespect begin, we make excuses for them. We fail to look at their involvement in every conflict they are involved in. We simply don't believe our lying eyes when who they are is presented in small ways at first.

When she snaps on you in front of your friends and then apologizes and blames it on stress at work, you accept it. When he says he's going to call and doesn't call, we accept that he got tied up. We overlook the fact that he doesn't call until the next afternoon. This is a sign that he will do this in the future. He has revealed how he will treat our relationship in the future, but we refuse to respond accordingly.

The problem with failing to respond accordingly is that the problem gets worse. The appropriate way to respond the first time is to have a conversation about the behavior and state your position about it. This is called setting a boundary or making your boundaries, needs, wants, desires known, whichever one is offended by the behavior.

If the behavior occurs again, we have to acknowledge that either the person can't do better or has no desire to do better. For our purposes, it does not matter which one -- can't or won't. Why? Because the behavior continues. This puts us in a position to have to make a choice that most of us, at this point, don't want to make. We have to either continue in the relationship or move on. We convince ourselves that this is too rash a decision to make. Nobody is perfect. As we move forward, having ignored a small warning sign, time is passing and we become more invested in the relationship. When it happens the next time, it is usually worse than the time before. The stakes get higher every time we ignore a warning sign that the person is not capable of respecting our boundaries and/or meeting our needs. Every step we take moving forward after justifying a violation of our boundaries is a step further we take on the Hurt People Highway toward Heartbreak Hotel.

I continued in a relationship where I was being treated like a queen in some ways, but disrespected in so many others. I could not understand why this relationship wasn't going to work. This had to be the man for me. The fact that he told me I was too much woman for him didn't matter. I thought he was *just saying that*. He was telling me the truth. I created an idol of him. I cared more for him than my own needs and wants. I was willing to sacrifice my dignity and self-respect. I was willing to allow him to be responsible only for those parts of me that he wanted to be responsible for. No matter how much pain and hurt I experienced, I allowed him to make it up to me. When I would try to get off the Highway, he would pursue me with everything he had. I would fall for it. I would allow him back in my life. Ultimately, it led me to the doors of Heartbreak Hotel.

I looked inside to see mental breakdown and thought it might not be that bad. At least it would stop the pain that I was in. Inside was a series of institutions. There were prisons, hospitals and cemeteries. These are the institutions that people check-in to when they check-in to the Heartbreak Hotel.

The most powerful emotion in the universe is love. When people love and they are hurt, the reactions vary but can be very dangerous, even explosive. Many people have stayed in relationships that were unhealthy in the name of love. Physically abusive relationships have led to the cemetery. Emotionally abusive relationships have led to the mental hospital. Physical and emotionally relationships have led to prison. People have committed murder in reaction to betrayal in love relationships. The criminal justice system even has a specific name for it -- crimes of passion.

It is important that we get off the Highway before we get to and check in to Heartbreak Hotel. We

How Do We Get Hurt?

are not meant to be in the kind of pain that we endure along the way. Often mental illness is the result of the brain simply detaching because it can no longer handle the pain and anguish. When we insist that we should remain in a relationship, despite the reality that it is not healthy and we are suffering as a result of being in the relationship, the pain intensifies with each betrayal, each new hurt. These are all signs, flashing neon lights, 2 x 4's to the head and even being run over by a truck, things that are meant to get our attention so that we will leave the situation. There are times that we have been shown that the relationship is not good for us, but we think that the other person needs us. So we stay. I call this the "messiah complex."

It is a first cousin to idol worship. Both are doomed to fail. There is but one savior for any of us. When we step in and, even though we have been shown that the relationship is not working for us, and worse, that we should leave the relationship, but we stay because we believe the other person needs us, they don't have anybody else in their lives, we have now stepped into the Creator's place and there is a price to pay for that.

I have seen people lose their lives trying to save someone else. They were disobedient to the warning signs that they admitted they had received that they should let the relationship go. They mentioned the warning to me on at least three occasions. They stayed. The person they believed needed them betrayed them in every way they could and left them eventually anyway. I know of a person who insisted that their mate needed them. I told them that self-preservation was a strong instinct and that their mate would be fine. The mate was on drugs and had become quite abusive. Well, lo and behold, the relationship ended. The person on drugs, within a year's time, was sober, working and driving a brand new Thunderbird. It turned out, he didn't need "saving."

The reason this is true is specifically because the Creator is the savior and when we go through harsh experiences, it leads us to Him. He will always be our savior. We don't need to do that for each other. We can support each other, but we are not each other's savior. So be very careful about insisting that you are the only person they have. We always have someone -- our Creator -- and that is sufficient for each of us.

It is actually quite arrogant to believe that another human being can't survive without you. I have heard it referred to as "getting in the way of the them and God." That is not a place that anyone should be in -- between another person and their God. It is definitely out of order, in someone else's lane, in the way even. Don't do it. There are consequences. The sooner we get out of the way, the sooner the Creator can do his work and the sooner the person you profess to love can be living their best life. Get out of the way. Besides, once the Creator has done his work on any of us, we are better for ourselves and the person we want to be with.

I have expended a lot of energy auditioning for a man. I showed him my talents in the kitchen, shared my knowledge and my body, all prior to him earning the privilege. As a young woman I wanted to make sure that the man knew that I was there for him and was not a gold-digger, I was understanding and a good woman. Little did I know that any man worth my time would find that out anyway because he would spend the time to find out. He would be there long enough to find out. If he left before he got to all of the good parts, it was because he was not worthy of me and my talents.

I had to learn not to audition for him. Simply be who I am and he would see the talents and the benefit of being with me. I don't need to lay out everything I have in the first few weeks to get a man's attention. First of all, the Creator took care of a lot of that. He gave me a pretty sexy body and an adorable face. Ok, nobody has to agree with me on this one, that is my story and I am sticking to it. Nobody can make me think otherwise.

In reality, however, if a man has expressed an interest in me, he saw something that got his attention already. I don't have to show him everything. He is there to investigate what he saw to see if he wants to know more. If he is interested he will spend the time to get to all of the things he wants to know about me and get from me, including sex, no matter how long it takes. Yes, men will wait for sex.

Remember, they love the chase. They love to hunt. They love to solve puzzles and problems. That

57

is what they do. Be the puzzle they have to figure out. It is a challenge and if they want to see the finished product, they will work to put the pieces together. If they lose interest along the way, then they were not the man for that puzzle.

There is nothing wrong with finding that out BEFORE you give them everything you have. I offer that we should be who we are at the beginning of the relationship and when the person we are interested in has invested enough in the relationship, that is when they are eligible to make withdrawals. When we make a deposit in the bank, it is not all available to us immediately, unless we have a balance on-hand already equal to or above the amount of the deposit. That means that until an investment of the size and magnitude of the withdrawal that we are attempting to make has ALREADY been made, we have to wait for access to those funds until the bank is assured that the funds are there. You can't go into the bank and hand the teller a pretty check and have access to that amount until it has been proven that the funds are actually available. In fact, it is called the "funds availability policy" at most banks. Well, we should be waiting until the person we are interested in has proven he or she has already invested and is available before we allow huge withdrawals from the bank of our heart.

No-one should have access to all of our time, talents, finances and certainly not our bodies until they have proven that they are invested and are available. This leads to another common stop along the highway that leads to hurt people:

• *Getting involved with someone who is already involved with someone else or because we think we can handle a purely sexual relationship with no strings attached.*

I see this mistake far too often. What makes anyone believe that they can "take" a person from the person they are with? What makes them think that they have something that the person they are with doesn't have? What makes a person think that if they cheat on or leave a person for you that they will not do the same *to* you.

In the case of a woman, there is no sex so great that a man will leave the woman he is with to be with another woman. He will accept the sex, but he is not leaving what he has. If the man wanted to leave the woman he is with, he simply would have already done so. Men don't need another woman to suddenly decide to leave the woman they are with. She may encourage him to add a woman, but he is not going to subtract one. He will have both.

For the add-on woman or side-chick, she has placed herself directly in harm's way. She is setting herself up for pain. It may come on the holidays he can't spend with you or the years you have wasted waiting for the children to grow up or the house to sell or the divorce papers to get filed. It may also come from the ass-whopping that the other woman will dispense once she finds out about you disrespecting her relationship.

No matter how it arrives, you have signed up for the hurt and pain. If you meet a man who is in a relationship with another woman, he does not have to be legally married to her or living with her, if he is

59
How Do We Get Hurt?

with another woman, the appropriate response to his advances is -- no thank you. As long as he is involved with someone else, he cannot be involved with you. I like to say that a man needs both his hands to handle me. There is no room for another person. I want what I want when I want it. I don't have time to wait on another woman's schedule to get the time and attention of the man I give myself to.

I also believe that I deserve better than the scraps of a man's time off of another woman's table. I am deserving of a full man. I have heard women say and men insinuate that a piece of man is better than no man at all. I strongly, with everything I have, disagree. I tried that "piece of man" thing and it led directly to the door of Heartbreak Hotel. Whenever he wanted to be with another woman, he simply started an argument with me, complained about me in some way so that he could justify not being with me to be with her. The problem is he never wanted to let me go completely. He wanted me to wait until he had his fill of the woman of the day.

All it led to was hurt for me. So I no longer want a piece of a man. I need all of him or I would rather have nothing of him. The only way I accept a piece of a man is if he is not an intimate partner and I manage how much time and friendship he gets. He is a friend and I don't have sex with my friends. That means that unless there is an emergency, he doesn't get to make late night or early morning phone calls. He doesn't get to come to my home unannounced. I don't put him before my rest, work, or other important things in my life. But he understands because he does not expect those things based on the nature of our relationship.

People often enter into sexual relationships that they say are just that -- purely sexual. There are no other strings attached. They are the late-night booty calls. The friends-with-benefits. Whatever. They are, by their very nature, not healthy. They usually only happen when one person decides it's time. Somebody always, eventually, wants more. The nature of what is being exchanged is so incredibly intimate and sacred that giving it away casually is almost certain to lead to somebody's feelings getting involved and ultimately, hurt. It is not always the woman who gets hurt in this arrangement. I know of more than one instance where the man wanted more and the woman wasn't willing to invest more. The man, just as with most women, didn't want to feel like a piece of meat and his feelings were hurt so he ended the arrangement. If you notice, I am calling this an arrangement. It would be use of the term "relationship" quite loosely to call the getting together simply for sex a relationship. Women are not designed to give the most precious gift they have to another person casually and without emotion.

Men don't like to feel that they are just a sex object, despite what some would have us believe. So these arrangements are destined to produce hurt. I have seen women that know the man has other sexual partners become irate that the man allowed them to see "signs" that the other woman had been there. I don't understand what difference it makes if that is the arrangement, but more than one woman has said

How Do We Get Hurt?

to me that they knew the man had other women but just didn't want it in their face.

Well, it, for me, is the reason I don't engage in sexual relationships with a man that I know has sex with other women. It is bound to hit me in the face at the most unfortunate time. It will hit on that date when I want to spend time with him and he can't. It could simply be that he has plans with his mother, but I will automatically assume it is another woman. When he doesn't answer my calls or text messages, it is another woman. It will always be another woman when I can't have him when I want him.

That does not have to be reality, but it will be how I process the fact that he is unavailable to me. This hurts my feelings. Bless the person who can withstand the pain that is built in with this situation. I have no interest in it. I'm clearly too mushy inside to handle the hurt. I don't like being in pain or angry. My friend says my threshold for pain is "zero tolerance." She must be right because if I even "think" engaging in this behavior is going to lead to pain, I will remove myself immediately.

I can't say this will work for everyone, but it is the way I have to handle my heart. I, after all, am the one responsible for the safe-keeping of my heart. It is no-one else's responsibility to guard my heart. I have assumed full responsibility to make sure that I don't, knowingly, put myself in harm's way. There may be a situation that a man lies to me and I find myself in a three-way relationship, but those kinds of lies are always exposed. I know that if a man is building his relationship with me on lies, if I keep my eyes open

How Do We Get Hurt?

and analyze his behavior objectively, something will alert me that something is not adding up.

Truth has a ring to it. Truth can stand up to scrutiny. If a man doesn't want me asking him questions about things that he says, for example, it is a sign that he is hiding something. Even if I don't know what it is, it is prudent for me to back up a little, go slow until I am sure what it is. We were all, men and women, blessed with instinct or intuition. When we use it, it protects us from hidden dangers that may lie ahead. The problem we face is that when we hear the warning signs, see those flags on the road, we don't trust the information. We would rather believe the lies -- the ones that sound like a lie when they are told -- than to trust what is coming from within us. This is a guaranteed ingredient in hurt. Trusting what someone else tells you over what your intuition tells you. Even when I have no proof for what my intuition tells me, I simply hold onto the information and watch for other signs that prove it. I begin to retreat my heart. I don't place all of my heart on the line if I suspect that something is not as it is being presented. However, if I am already sexually involved, it will cloud the sound of intuition. It makes it harder for me to hear the sounds. I am too busy with my eyes closed yelling ooh oooh oooohhh!

We have to trust what comes from within because that is where the Creator lives, moves and has His being. This is the most reliable source of information. However, it is the last thing we are told to trust. Society tell us to trust only what we see. Well, I lean more heavily on what comes from within. It has been right more often than not. We have all experienced that time when "something told me. . ." You can fill in the blank. When we listened to that "something," things worked out. When we didn't listen, things did not turn out well. Still, as many times as that has been proven true, we trust anything other than our intuition or that still, small voice within us. It is the trick of the opposition to get us to listen to anything other than the source that will lead us to the right answer for us, the answer that will bring us good results and peace.

Now, I strongly believe that two consenting adults can consent to whatever they want to. I have no place to judge what two adults agree to. I can only speak on those things that I know for sure. I know for sure that entering an arrangement that calls for me to give up the most precious gift I have to a person that has no responsibility to me is a recipe for me to get hurt. I don't handle hurt well. Hurt, over anger, makes me want to fight. Hurt brings out the crazy-broad in me. I don't like her. She is really crazy and disrespectful. She is the one who wants to break out windows, put sugar in gas tanks, you know the crazy one. I try to keep her in check. I keep her under the sewer like a Ninja Turtle. She will wear my clothes and do things in my name that I have no memory of. She wreaks havoc over my life in my body, clothes and probably driving my car. But she needs to be in an institution. She is hurt. Hear her roar. Better yet, let's NOT see her at all. How do I keep her in check? I don't engage in situations involving my heart that I know can lead to hurt. Why? Because hurt people hurt people. I am no exception to that rule. If you hurt me, I am subject to hurt back. Proceed with caution.

How Do We Get Hurt?

- *The key is to get off before you check in to Heartbreak Hotel*

The Highway leading to Heartbreak Hotel is paved with a lot of pain, anguish, betrayal, loss, fear, self-doubt, abandonment and other painful emotions. I know there are pieces of my skin and stains from my blood on the Highway. I travelled that Highway all the way to the door and looked in through the window before I realized I had to get off that road. It is amazing how it works. Once you have been down that Highway as far as I traveled it, when you get off, you vow never to follow that Highway that long again. When you see the signs that you have entered that Highway or someone is asking you to pay a toll on that bridge, you recognize it, an all-too-familiar feeling comes over you and you know it's time to change roads. Lauren Hill has a song titled *Ex-Factor*. In the song, she has a line that says: "Cause no one's hurt me more than you and no-one ever will."

Once I had experienced that kind of hurt, I vowed never to experience it again. It meant that I had to evaluate the relationship from beginning to end to see how it got so bad. How did I become susceptible to such pain? That is when I had to look at ME first. It was not sufficient to look at the other person. In fact, I never would have been able to resolve the hurt and pain unless I looked inwardly. It is always easier to look at the behavior of other people instead of looking so much closer -- straight in the mirror at ourselves.

When I analyze any relationship challenge, the first place I look is at me. All of the answers are *in me*. Even the answers to why another person did what they did *to* me. How is that possible? Because of something I shared earlier, no-one can do to you what you do not allow them to do in a relationship. The answer is always the same -- because you let them. Believe me, there were signs that this big betrayal was coming, that this person had character flaws that could lead to this kind of hurt. I simply continued on the Highway, ignoring the warning signs that worse danger was ahead.

Heck, every state highway patrol puts out signs weeks in advance that there is going to be road work done in the near future and you should expect delays. When they are working for a day or two they put up bright orange or red signs saying there is road work being done ahead, slow down, there is the potential for danger not just to your car, but possibly to the people doing the work. Be alert.

In fact, you may need to take a detour. Well, the Hurt People Highway has all of those warning signs too. Just like the regular highway signs, some of them are just hand-held flags -- this is something to pay attention to in the future. Some warnings are bigger flags posted well ahead of the potential danger -- this is going to be a problem. Some are electronic signs with dates telling you to expect delays and even giving you alternate routes to avoid the area altogether -- these are the signs that advise you that you have a serious problem to resolve before major damage is done. It is asking you to seriously consider getting out of the situation altogether.

Now, there are still other signs that say the road will be closed for a period of time. You can continue on the road beyond each of these signs and warnings. However, you do so *by your own choice*. The fact that you continue beyond the signs and your car picks up a nail in the tire or worse, is not the department of transportation's fault. They warned you that there was a potential danger. The fact that you are now late for your appointment is not the fault of the road workers, it is your fault. You participated. You continued on when you had that "feeling something wasn't right."

I recognize that people can be harmed by strangers and be devastated by these acts. However, the betrayals that cause the deepest hurt are the ones where we believed we were in a relationship with the person who hurt us. This is because they are the people we trusted, the ones we allowed in our hearts. They were family and were supposed to love us. Those are the hurts that cause the deepest scars. They are also the hardest to recover from.

But I offer that the process should be the same, no matter who the offending person is. When we see that family members are treating us with disrespect, taking advantage of us, lying to us, disappointing us time and time again, it is time to love them from a distance. There is no rule in the "family handbook" that requires us to subject ourselves to harmful treatment because we share a bloodline.

The key to avoiding Heartbreak Hotel's institutions is to stop participating in relationships that cause hurt so deep that we want to hurt in return. I hear all of the people saying how complicated things are when it involves an intimate or familial relationship. I have found, upon further investigation when people tell me this, that the truth is the choices are quite clear, it is not complicated at all. It is simply that we do not *like* the choices and are looking for another way to stop the hurt or get what we want. We want the parts of the situation we want to keep. We want the things that we feel benefit us, knowing that the things that hurt us will not end.

We, unfortunately, can't have it both ways. When it has been made clear that we are at that fork in the road, we know if we continue in the direction we have been going, it is going to lead to more pain and is not likely to stop producing hurt and pain, and we have only two choices: stay or leave.

Whichever one we choose, we own the results. The key is to get out of situations that lead to wanting to hurt people before we get to that point. It may not be what we want to do, but it is the healthiest thing for everyone involved. We were not designed to withstand extended pain and hurt. This is where people break with reality and become mentally ill because the brain refuses to continue to accept the pain and hurt. It simply does what we have not had the courage to do -- it just stops participating. The brain is an amazing organ. There is a lot we can learn from it and the rest of the body.

How Do We Get Hurt?

Chapter 3

LOVE
INCARCERATED

**"Sometimes we live in a prison of our own making.
Sometimes, we even like it there."**

• *We ain't gotta be mad*

In the classic Gladys Knight & The Pips song, *Neither One Of Us,* they sing a song that describes perfectly why we stay in relationships that are not good for us. At some point, Gladys says *there is no way this can have a happy ending.* We have convinced ourselves that there is no way a relationship can come to a "happy ending" so we go on hurting each other and pretending to the world that it is ok. I know people that have stayed in unhappy, unhealthy marriages for decades pretending for the world that the relationship is good. All the while hurting. It is this belief that has caused so many so much hurt. We ain't got to be mad to get out!

When my relationship with a man who had been incarcerated ended, I was hurt, but I wasn't angry. I had so long ago learned that I don't have to be disagreeable, angry, bitter and hurt to leave a relationship that is not working for me. I can simply just walk away. The other person doesn't have to be "bad" for us to part ways. I don't have to be "bad" for the best choice to be ending the relationship. I have learned not to take this personally. I have also learned and practiced with great success that there doesn't have to be an explanation about the final act or the thing that made me come to the conclusion that it is finally time to end the relationship.

Whenever I have ended a relationship, I have communicated to the person that I am in a relationship with those things that don't work for me during the relationship. I don't hold onto transgressions or things that offend me and wait until an argument to express them. I am a firm believer that no-one can know how or what I feel unless I *tell them*. One of my least favorite statements is: well he/she should already know. How exactly can they know if you haven't said anything? I want to be certain that the other person understands the "what and why" of how I am feeling. If I am offended I tell them so that they know not to do it again. If they persist, then I bring it to their attention.

Typically, I do not continue in a relationship where the offensive behavior continues beyond the third or fourth time before I end the relationship, unless it is behavior that I intend to accept as a continuing part of the relationship. That behavior has to be something that I have thought about and

Love Incarcerated

decided I can live with. I recognize that whatever I get in the beginning is when the person is trying to impress me and that anything that I see, I have to expect it to be worse later.

Getting to know me is not going to cause a person to miraculously change their character. It will simply reveal what was always there. The longer we are in relationships, the more comfortable people become and the more their true character and nature reveals itself. But when the relationship is over, I do not have a need to "get closure" by telling them what they did wrong and why I am leaving. I just leave. In my opinion, the only reason for further discussion is if I am trying to salvage the relationship. If I am truly done, why do I need to explain and the "closure" already happened. The idea of closure is another seemingly acceptable reason to talk about a relationship you are not done with. Don't take my word for it, examine the times you wanted to talk to the person to gain closure. I'll wait. Uh huh!!!

Expecting a person to become a different person -- in short, change who they are -- because they are in a relationship with you is a misguided notion. The only person we can change, and that, if we are lucky, is us. I believe change in the structure of a person only happens when they have made a conscious effort and it has to be accompanied by direct intervention from a power higher than mere humans. In working in the prison, I have worked with people who are actively trying to change themselves for the better. They are trying to rehabilitate their view of the world and their place in it. This is a difficult process. It requires breaking

71

down whatever we know about ourselves and rebuilding it. It is easier to form something out of a substance that has never been formed than to undo what has already been formed and allowed to harden.

The saying you can't teach an old dog new tricks comes to mind. It's not that you can't, you just have to have a power higher than you to assist. The subject has to want that kind of substantive change. So proceeding in a relationship thinking that the obstacles you see today are miraculously going to disappear just with the passage of time is unwise. Chances are, those obstacles will grow larger and play a larger part in the relationship. This is why I believe once I am aware that there is behavior that the other person has engaged in that is a likely deal-breaker for me on more than two occasions, I have to make a choice whether to stay or go right then.

Sometimes, because I know that nobody is perfect and their good traits and behavior outweigh the behavior I don't like, I decide to accept the offending behavior as one of those things I will simply have to live with being with this person. At that point, I discontinue bringing it up. In other words, I won't nag about the behavior. I have, of my own will, accepted behavior that is less than what I would desire. This category of behavior can only be minor offenses for me. I don't expect to like every trait about a person but I also don't expect to have to endure hurt and pain consistently and regularly to have a relationship.

This is probably because I enjoy the first relationship I have, the one between me and my Creator. While I have spent significant time single, as

Love Incarcerated

the world views it, I prefer that to being in a bad relationship. Let me say this here. I was fortunate to get over shame over a failed relationship in my twenties. I felt shame that this relationship that, on paper, appeared to have all the ingredients to be successful was failing me. I was not happy because, as I was later able to articulate for myself, I had no position, no title, no right to require anything because I had agreed to participate in this relationship without those things. Because the relationship lasted for years, I felt foolish admitting to myself, and certainly those around me, that I was not considered this man's girlfriend. I was just a friend! After years, that was it? Yup. I was embarrassed. I was ashamed.

When I no longer wanted it to be that way, I didn't have the courage to simply get out for good. I attempted to end the relationship a few times during those years. Every time I would try to end the relationship, he would pursue me with a vengeance. He would "throw me a bone." He would do something that he knew I wanted to bring me back into the relationship. He would pursue and I would volunteer to go back into the incarceration of a relationship that was not meeting my needs. While it was going on, I thought I was having fun. It was not until I had truly, completely removed myself and engaged in another relationship that I realized just how *little* fun I was having and that I had wasted quite a bit of time in a relationship that wasn't working for me.

It is relevant to note that I knew then and I know now, that the man loved me dearly. The reason the relationship wasn't working had nothing to do with whether or not he loved me. The problem was that he was not ready to be in the kind of relationship that I wanted. He wanted to have access to me whenever he wanted without a responsibility to be there when I wanted him to be.

He was not obligated to meet my needs. This was a form of prison I accepted. When I decided enough was enough, I was ashamed. Then I thought about that. Who was I ashamed in front of? Why? I didn't know anyone who had not had a failed relationship. Why was I ashamed in front of any of them? It helped me to understand, relatively early in my life, that people don't engage in relationships or not, based on what I think and feel about them. Everybody I know stays or leaves a relationship based on their own choices. They don't consult me and decide just because I said stay or go. People have choices and they use them based on their feelings, not mine. I have seen lots of situations that I think are unhealthy and unfulfilling to the people in them but they choose that and it is not up to me to decide if their choice is a "good or bad" one. Even if it is not the choice I think I would make given the same set of circumstances, it doesn't matter. The person will know soon enough if it is a bad choice.

When I fell in love with a man that was fifteen years younger and incarcerated, it took me by surprise. It went against things I said I would not do, like visiting a man in prison. This was something I said in my teens I would not subject myself to, having visited a family member in prison and been traumatized by the *process*. Yet, I could not wait to visit this man in prison. When he was incarcerated, the feelings grew over a period of a little over a year. I was amazed that after all he had been through in his life, that he still had a loving, caring heart. Not just toward me, but toward the other inmates, his family and people in general.

To me, that spoke volumes about his capacity to love. He loved me. It did not hurt that he was drop-dead gorgeous and a man's man. However, just prior to him leaving prison, he expressed concern about the demons that would be waiting for him when he got home. He was clear about what he wanted, but had no illusions about the reality that he was weak to certain things.

When he came home and things did not work between us, I was not angry about it. I was sad that it didn't work out the way I hoped it would. However, before it got to the point that I was hurt to the point of hurting back, I removed myself. What this allowed me to do was to cherish the things that I received in the relationship that were good. It was a blessing that he did not stay. It was a blessing that I had experienced love without fear. It was a gift that I will always cherish.

As such, I am not mad, but I didn't allow myself to be trampled, at least not for long. When I felt that I was not being treated the way that I should, I made the hard choice not to participate. The breakup happened over and over again for a period of about a year. I know that sounds crazy, but it did. He would leave at the end of a perfectly good time and I may not hear from him for a while. He would reemerge and we would spend time as friends. More often than not, we were not sexual when he returned.

I was always glad that he did not attempt to have sex with me on these returns because it would have made me feel used. But instead, he would call and we would spend time together. We always had a good time in each other's company. In my mind, no harm, no foul. Again, I wasn't angry at him, so there was no restriction on me spending time with him. It was not until I felt that he disregarded my feelings and needs that I stopped participating. He was shocked when he called and I told him I did not want to see him. It was a gift that he respected me and did not pursue me when I said I did not want to participate anymore. He was clear about who he was NOT and it was a gift to me to leave me alone.

The point for sharing all of this is to say that it was not complicated. The relationship was not complicated. The choice to get out was not complicated. I did not want to make the choice, but in the spirit of self-preservation, it was what was required. In taking the steps necessary to protect my heart from hurt and pain, I have been able to preserve the love I have for him and cherish the memories of the extremely good times we had. It also leaves open the possibility that if he ever makes changes of his own free will that enables him to treat me the way I deserve to be treated, then I may have the relationship.

I did not allow so much damage to be done to me or the relationship that the door has to be permanently closed. I do not look at anything that I did for him as him taking advantage of me because I consciously -- during the time it was going on -- only did what I wanted to do. It was part of the gift of

Love Incarcerated

loving without fear. I didn't care what it looked like or if it was perceived that I was being used. I did what made me happy to do for him. When I sent him packages to the prison, it was because I asked him how I could and I did it. When I had sex with him, it was because I wanted to. When I rented a car for him to get to his job as a union ironworker, it was because I wanted to. It would have been disingenuous of me, after it was over, to scream that he took advantage of me by allowing me to do things that I offered to do, without him asking me to do them. I did not consider it being used to do what I wanted to and was in a position to do for someone that I loved and knew needed help.

Some people feel used, but I could not allow it to be said that he was guilty of something that simply wasn't true. I participated with my eyes wide open. Those things also made me feel good. I got something out of doing for the man that I loved. It was a wonderful feeling that I still cherish. Heck, I get enjoyment out of giving. People that know me will attest to that. I have learned wisdom over the years, however. Not everyone is worthy of receiving and therefore, I use a little more discretion. If I ever sense that a person feels entitled to receiving, that is a deal-breaker for me. I stop giving to them. This is not how everyone should operate, it is simply how I am happiest and fulfilled.

If a person offers to do something for you that you need done, how do you become a user for accepting the help? I don't see how that label applies. There were so many times that he resisted my help too. He wanted to do for himself. He wanted to succeed on his own. Real men always do. However, I know that there is no-one who succeeds alone. Everyone needs help to succeed somewhere along the way. Everyone. I remind the men in the halfway house that everybody needs help at some point and that there is no shame in accepting it. In fact, it is wise to seek help when it's needed, especially if it is being offered. Despite the many challenges that he did have, he endeavored to be a man and stand on his own. It taught me a valuable lesson. I can not do too much for a man. It made him feel "less than." It messed with his manhood. His way of dealing with this was to disappear. He would return, but he would have to get out of my presence for a while. I was a reminder of his shortcomings. Let's face it, nobody wants a constant reminder of their inadequacy. It is a source of pain for all of us.

When I began to feel that he was taking my kindness for weakness and disregarding my feelings, I stopped the interaction altogether. It is important to say here again, that I was not angry. I simply took the actions necessary as they presented themselves. When he called and asked if I wanted to see him, the answer was no. When he asked if I missed him, the answer was no. I truly did not, I'm not into being hurt or disregarded.

The last time I saw him he asked me if he got his stuff together would I be with him. I could honestly tell him that "if" he got himself together I would. How could I know in that moment? I knew because the love was real and I enjoyed his company. We have a chemistry that is undeniable. It's like asking someone that loves motorcycles "if" things work out the way I want them to, will you accept a Harley-Davidson with all the bells and whistles from me? Do they really have to think about that for long? No. They don't because they already know that if things work out, they would be thrilled to have a top-of-the-line motorcycle.

I stopped the interaction because I refused to allow, even him, to do damage to the love and memories I had of this relationship. I have some of the sweetest memories of that relationship. We seemed to function in sync when together. If we went somewhere, invariably, when I was ready to leave, as soon as I had the thought, within minutes he would ask if I would be ready to leave soon. There was an ease to being together. I never, not from the very beginning, felt that I needed to be someone different to please him. He made me feel totally enough from the beginning. It was liberating. My heart was locked down though. I didn't need or want anyone else. I had his heart. I know I still do, even though we don't talk. I feel him so often. I am happy to have had the experience. I learned a lot from the relationship about managing how much of me to invest in a relationship and when it is acceptable to do that.

One priceless lesson cemented how my relationship with my father affected me in relationships with men. I realized that the man I was in love with was very similar to my father in his attitudes and treatment of me and other people. It occurred to me while I was visiting my father in hospice care a few months before he died. I had gone to Montana to visit him while he was still coherent and could talk. We decided that that would be better than waiting until he was no longer able to speak. He had pancreatic cancer, which is common for people that have had diabetes for a long time. It was certain at his age that he would die from the disease. While visiting him, I witnessed an exchange between him and a friend he had been close to for the past 13 years. The man was supposed to handle his affairs. The man did not listen to my father's wishes and my father told him that he was no longer going to have him handle his affairs. It was not so much what he said, but the way he said it and how quickly he dismissed him. My father tossed him aside with a quickness.

For some reason, that exchange gave me a glimpse of what it looked like with my guy. He had not developed a ton of coping skills throughout his life. The two that everyone are born with were intact, however: fight or flight. Since he would not fight me, when he was not feeling what was happening, he took flight. His view of the world, due to having been mistreated in prison and in life, was very specific. Certain things required a person to be cut off, immediately.

Both men were very definite in their assessment and response. Many people would do good to adopt a little of this trait. When you see danger on the Highway, get off before you get there. With them, it was not an emotional conversation. It just had to be that way.

In the situation with my father and his friend, I could see that the man was hurt. My father dismissed him in front of my niece and I. To be clear, the man was violating my father's wishes. I had also observed that he had no recognition for the fact that my father had to adjust to the reality that he was dying. This man was former military and he treated the situation with military precision. He was moving too fast to dismantle my father's life for my father to adjust to the reality. The problem with that approach is that it was my father's life! The situation required a little more finesse. My father was not dead yet. He was *dying*. He still wanted to make his own decisions for as long as he could. He had earned that. Once a person is free from being dictated to, they are sensitive to having someone else make decisions for and about their life.

My father had survived an addiction. An addiction that cost him his family, his freedom for a short period of time, his dignity and so much more. When he regained control over his life, he certainly, even with death at his door, was not going to cede that power to another person. Not as long as he had breath.

I had seen the same conviction in my man. More than anything however, was the similarity in the sense that they never really could be totally free with their emotions in a relationship. With both men, I knew for sure that they loved me. Both told me as much regularly. Both expressed affection with me easily. Both men treated me like a queen when I was in their presence. Both men would withhold their time and attention from me if they were upset without explanation.

With both men, I had a connection, so I could feel them without ever having to have a conversation with them about what was going on. Like the New Year's Eve phone call, I felt so compelled to make to my father at such a young age. With my man, there were times when he was incarcerated that I knew he was experiencing dis-ease and upset. Even though we were not together when his mother passed away, I knew something was upsetting him. I reached out to him and learned that his mother had passed away. The connection and love was real in both relationships.

Both men had their emotional development stunted due to cards they were dealt in the course of their lives. It impacted their ability to express their emotional thoughts in words. It caused them to withdraw emotionally very quickly. This was the case, despite how freely they showed affection and expressed in words their love. Both men were openly affectionate with their children. Both men told their children that they loved them regularly. However, when things bothered them in their lives, both men withdrew from their children and loved ones.

Sitting in the hospice facility in Montana, talking to my loved on the phone about my father, it hit me that the two men were very much alike. I had never connected that before, but it became crystal clear to me, that they were very similar and most importantly *how* they were similar. It opened a door of understanding for me that I consistently got involved with men who were loving but had trouble opening up due to their past experiences. It rendered them emotionally unavailable to me when I needed them. I am so grateful to have gained that understanding. Now I am able to see it ahead of time and make better choices.

With both men, I always considered what they had been through when evaluating their treatment of me. I always gave them a pass for their emotional challenges. I factored their life's experiences in when looking at their behavior. What I learned is that it is all right to look at their life's experiences, but that is not a justification to let them off the hook of responsibility to care for me and meet my needs.

Obviously, the nature of the needs was different between the two men, but my approach to my man was informed by the approach I developed with my father as a young girl. I put his issues before my own. I allowed him to withdraw and return because I knew the withdrawal did not mean that he didn't love me. He always made sure to remind me just how much he loved me and how blessed he was to have me in his life. He expressed appreciation for my understanding.

However, none of that stopped me from hurting when he disappeared. None of that could erase the fact that I would spend another holiday alone. None of that erased the disappointment of cancellations when we planned to go somewhere together. My response, from the beginning, should have been to require more from them. I should not have always been understanding of their issues. Even in understanding, I could have expressed that I understood but required them to fulfill their commitments to me. I learned that I have to set up the requirements early. No matter how much I understand a man's plight, if he can't be consistent and responsible with my needs, then he should not have access to my talents, gifts and time. It is a

Love Incarcerated

priceless lesson that I am glad I learned. For this alone, I am not angry that I was in the relationship. I gained priceless insight into myself. It informs my choices now.

- *It doesn't have to be a bad thing that the season changed*

So often people want to get out of a relationship that they are not happy in but nothing has happened any different from what has been happening. No major event has occurred, so they continue to do what they have been doing. As an employer for many years, I have experienced it over and over again. Employees create some conflict between themselves and another co-worker or their supervisor to make them feel justified in leaving. I have seen some even do things that they knew would get them fired instead of simply giving a two-week notice and resigning their position.

I have often felt that they just couldn't break off the employment relationship without a fight, stating a reason to leave, or making someone in the company a villain. Personal relationships are often the same, probably even more so. People don't want to admit that the relationship simply is no longer working for them or the other party. There is a very true statement: Some people come into our lives for a reason, some for a season and some for a lifetime.

Our natural inclination is to want the intimate partner that we have to be the one for a "lifetime." Well, it is also true that not every intimate relationship we have is going to last a lifetime. It does not have to be a bad thing because the season in our lives for this particular relationship has ended. Once we have learned what we can from a relationship, it may end. There may be something that the other person needed to learn from us and our job in that position ended. Know this, it is always to make room for something much better. At the end of the most hurtful relationship I have ever experienced, I distinctly remember thinking that this was a terrible thing because I would never find sex as good as I had with that man.

The truth is that the best sex I have ever had happened after the end of that relationship. Not only did I experience the best sex I ever had after that relationship, but the best relationship I ever had occurred after that relationship. So at this point, if I see that a relationship is not fulfilling, I don't believe I have to create a crisis to walk away. I don't need a man to get busted cheating on me, abuse me physically or mentally or not support me financially to end the relationship if it is not fulfilling to me or the other person. I ended the best relationship I have experienced to date because I saw in the person's face that he was no longer happy to see me at the end of the day.

I noticed that my finances were suffering, not because this person ever asked me for money. For some reason though, my bank account would be overdrawn just before payday. I had not bounced a check in decades. I firmly believe that if things are not going well in my life that I am required to examine every area of my life to find the thing that is out of balance, unhealthy, out of whack and fix it.

Love Incarcerated

I learned from the most painful experience I ever had, to look at myself first as the source of challenges. What am I doing to cause or contribute to the situation that I perceive as having a negative impact? I have to say the situation that "I perceive to be negative" because I usually learn great lessons even in negative situations and, as I said before, they tend to be making way for my better situation. So when my bank account would be overdrawn and nothing was visibly different about my spending habits or the amount of bills I had, I knew that I needed to pay close attention to what was happening around me. One night I walked into the house and the look on his face when I said hello was not good. I realized at that moment that the season for that relationship had ended. I was not mad about it. I knew I had not been totally fulfilled in the relationship for a while, but I was not miserable. But when I looked in his face and realized he was not happy with me, I knew it was time for it to end. I had a conversation with him very quickly and set a date that he would leave. I firmly believed that if neither of us were happy, there was no point to us remaining together. I believe that the negative energy was affecting my finances.

There is simply no reason to remain incarcerated in a painful relationship. If we do, it is because we have chosen that incarceration. For anyone who has ever been incarcerated by the penal system, I am sure that they would not willingly return to that prison unless they have decided to give up on life. There are a few people that have been incarcerated for so long that they find it difficult to reintegrate back into civilian life. They may choose to re-offend so that they can return to the life they know. These people have a mental conditioning that makes this seem logical.

Well, if you decide to return or remain incarcerated in a relationship that is filled with hurt, there is a mental conditioning that bears understanding. Understand that it is of your own free will and you can no longer play victim. I want to be mentally conditioned so that I keep a get-out-of-jail-free card in my pocket at all times just in case I wake up and realize I've been slipping.

Chapter 4

RELEASING THE PAIN

I've been going over it in my mind a thousand times. How did I end up here? When you were gone I thought I did it all right. I held you down. I had all the tools. I made my list and checked it twice. J Pay – check, Global Tel-link account for the home and cell phone – check check, Secure Pac account – check, approved visitor form – check, and of course a fresh book of stamps – check. I got a camera and lots of photo paper so I don't even have to go to the drug store to print out the latest family flics. I got a job so I send cash when you need it and put gas in the car for the long-ass ride to come see you. I got my patience to get me through the lottery and security at the visitor's gate, I got my understanding of the fact that you can't be here to hold me at night when I'm feeling down. I got compassion for the fact that you got caught up in the system in the first place.

I don't hold it against you cause I know they stacked the deck against you before "your daddy" was born. I got my love, dedication and commitment. I kept my battery supply so I could keep it tight and right just for you. *My days are scheduled around your calls. But it was all worth it cause you called regularly, when I had a hard day, your letters would be waiting. I got birthday cards, Christmas, Valentine's and Mother's Day cards. I was on top of the world cause YOU loved ME. It made me better. I walked with a spring in my step, a sway in my back and a smile in my heart. The world was mine – what??? It didn't matter that most of these relationships don't work. Hell, like you said, we know what it is. We ain't playin' no games here.*

I counted the days until you came home. Ninety days, sixty days, thirty days, oh shit a week. I can't even breathe. I pack my bags and make my reservations so I can pick you up at the gate. My man can't ride no bus. I gotta be there so he knows. . .I got your back. I think I proved it already, but just in case, I'm here. I got your favorite things and your favorite drink on ice. Nothing's too good for this day.

I see the van and know that you're a few feet away. I'm shaking. I can hardly catch my breath. I'm praying that nothing goes wrong. I've been waiting a long time for this day. Finally – you're home! I finally get to cook for you, turn them tricks I told you about, taste the wine of your presence, feel the divine. But that's not what happened.

See I forgot that hurt people hurt people. I forgot that if you don't know and love yourself, there's no way you can know and love me. See I thought the only thing between us and our happiness were the walls. But I didn't know that the walls were a blockade against your fears and insecurities. See you KNEW YOUR PLACE behind the walls. Behind the walls you were confident and sure. You were the sexiest man alive because you knew. You even dared to dream a dream. The walls were the security blanket that kept your manhood in check.

Releasing the Pain

But now you're not sure. In fact, you're insecure. In this world, you don't know who you are. It makes you mean. You can't commit to me cause you can't commit to this "you" you don't know. I realize you're hurting. It hurts you not to be able to provide, to have to accept help, not to have your own. So the hurt plays on. . . I'm hurt and confused every time you stand me up, don't call when you say you will, refuse to spend time with me, sit in a room and refuse to talk, withhold sex from me, start hanging with those same people you said you wouldn't, return to the things that took you from me in the first place. Oh and let's not forget the signs of the bitches that can't wear my flip flops, much less my Gucci boots, that you fuck wit to make you feel like a man again.

I'm devastated hurt when you tell me to go find somebody else if I can't handle it. How the hell do I do that? You got my heart on lock down. I don't even know where to look. I've been too busy proving my love for you, waiting for you, being understanding, being patient. What the fuck do you mean? Are you serious? But I know you are. In an odd way, you tell me that because you truly love me. You know you're afraid you can't make it. You don't want me to hang around to see what you perceive is inevitable failure. I know – you lie to be cause you care. Jody my Jody.

Yes, your manly philosophy is fucked up and in full effect. So stop disrespecting me by disregarding my time and feelings. Hurt. Stop making me feel like everything and everybody comes before me. Hurt. Since I'm understanding, I'm always the first in line for disappointment. Hurt. I'm the one that sent the packages, accepted the collect calls, saved the pussy!!!

You said you would protect and take care of me. But why am I here alone on yet another holiday. Why aren't you here at the end of a long day? Where you at - -Jennifer

Releasing the Pain

Hudson? Why are you neglecting me? How did I wind up here? Alone, confused, hurt? How did I get here? Oh – that's right. It was that road travelled so often by so many before. The road from confident, strong, beautiful black man behind the walls through the gates of panic, self-doubt, fear, insecurity to full-blown identity crisis. I took that ride with you down that dark road. I should have asked the conductor to stop somewhere along the way and got off, but I kept holding on to the poles of stabilization that were your letters, cards and promises. I know he's in there. You look the same, you talk the same, you even laugh the same – whenever I get to hear it. But its all a mirage cause you don't know who the hell you are. But I love you still. My love, the currency of exchange, the price of admission to that crowded highway of hurt people that leads to hurt people. Got to be more careful.

The poem you just read is a poem that was written about my experience in a relationship with a man incarcerated and what happened upon his release. I had never written anything before, other than papers for school, but certainly not a piece of spoken word. A friend told me "Yahweh told me to tell you to write your pain, you are going to help a lot of people with it." I had no idea how to do that, but was determined to obey the commands of Yahweh. I am not a church-going Christian, but I live every moment of my life trying to be in-step with the universal spirit law that I know controls everything. So I decided to write. This was one of the steps to releasing the pain of the relationship failing. It is really important for me to say here that this, fortunately for me, was not a devastating pain. I had learned in my twenties how to avoid being devastated by a relationship and its ultimate demise.

The pain from that relationship lasted months on end, day and night. As I explained, it took me to the door of Heartbreak Hotel and I looked in and thought it might not be that bad. This pain was real, but it never became overwhelming.

There are two distinct reasons for this that I can identify. The first reason was my behavior: I did not do anything in that relationship that I did not want to do, with my eyes wide open. I did not sit as a doormat without expressing my feelings and needs. This was so, even when I showed understanding about his circumstance. I always stated how I felt during the relationship. The second thing that kept the pain from becoming overwhelming was the behavior of my man. He would disappear -- totally. He did not call me to talk or show up at my office or home. His absence allowed me to gain perspective every time he would disappear. It was a blessing. When the final break came, he simply has not called me again nor shown up in any place that I frequent. I know that he still cares, because he frequently expresses this to a family member that tells me every time I see her. However, his absence has always given me the space I need to heal from whatever amount of pain I was feeling. I was not subjected to the death of my heart from a thousand cuts. My heart was bruised for sure, but not cut up in little pieces or crushed into ashes, as it had been when I thought about checking into Heartbreak Hotel.

There are certain things that I have learned along the way that help release the pain of any relationship. It is critical to release the pain. Otherwise, it begins to kill you and not the other person. Holding on to grudges, hurts, offenses, betrayals and pain -- no matter how big you perceive them to be -- is destructive to our mental and physical health. It is NOT, however, destructive to the person that committed any of the offenses.

For those folks that subscribe to the philosophy "don't get made, get even," the best way to do that is to live your best life. When you live your best life, the other person has not succeeded, whether intentionally or unintentionally, in destroying your joy. An added benefit is that when you live your best life, you are happy and it shows. It makes you a magnet for other good things and other good relationships of all kinds. It is the universal law of attraction. If you are in pain, reliving the betrayal, focusing on the wrongs that have been done to you from every failed relationship, you will attract more people that will continue the cycle because you are bringing into your life that which you spend the bulk of your time focusing on. It is inevitable. There is no way around it. Guard your thoughts as if your life depends on it -- because it does. What you focus on becomes your life.

Another reason it is imperative that we release the pain from previous relationships is that it prevents us from seeing every action of every person in our lives as the same actions that caused us so much pain. Men and women both accumulate baggage from relationships that they carry into the next relationship. It is unavoidable that we have memory of anything that we consider bad that has happened in a previous relationship. The key is not to project everything we have been through onto the next person.

I know a man who had a long-term relationship with a woman and he judges every woman by the poor character of the woman he spent many years with. The truth is he did not give what he wanted to receive and he accepted poor treatment based on some pseudo-honorable principle. The reality was that he did not believe he deserved any better and was not willing to give or be better so he stayed in a relationship where he and the woman treated each other poorly and inflicted constant pain on each other. He then accused every woman he knew, even women he was not in an intimate relationship with, of being just like her. He would make these generalizations about how women act. They were all based on her character. Not every woman is the same in every aspect. There are so many variables to how a woman functions in a relationship with a man, that it is a foolish notion to assume you already know how every woman is going to respond based on a previous relationship.

That makes me think of a funny story. A man I was dating, and I use that term very loosely, told me that he liked a perfume I wore, but would not tell me which one. When I asked him why he wouldn't tell me which scent he liked, he told me that he was not going to tell me because if he did, then I would wear that perfume all the time. This was very funny to me because it assumes that I wear my perfume *for him*. I wear perfume for me. I wear makeup, for me. I wear the kind of clothes I wear, for me.

It is very nice and I certainly enjoy it when other people, especially the man I am involved with, appreciate my efforts. But my reason for wearing perfume is about me. This is a news flash for those men who don't already know this: not everything women do is about or for you!

The interesting thing is that this man had known me for at least ten years and I am sure that if you ask him, he probably can never think of a time when I did not wear perfume regularly. I like my smell-good. It makes me happy. I owned and wore the perfume he liked before he started coming around. That is how he knew he liked it. I was wearing it. Duh! I did not always wear makeup, however. I have gone through phases. I am a girly girl. I love playing with colors and I love to see the enhancement of my best features. It makes me smile.

However, when I was working on a construction site full-time, the dirt flying and such made it impossible to wear makeup. I would get in my car at the end of the day and realize that I had mascara smeared all around my eyes making me look like a raccoon. I decided that it wasn't worth it and stopped. The only makeup I always wore was lipstick. That was not so much about looking good as much as it was about keeping my lips from being chapped. I hate chapped lips.

In recent years, I was producing a concert and my friend told me she was going to have a makeup artist do our makeup for the show. I protested, but by the time the makeup artist arrived, I was so glad to be sitting down, I went for it. I knew enough to know that I did not want raccoon eyes from too much concealer under my eyes. She assured me that she knew how to blend it all so that it looked natural. It was "just an enhancement." It was so relaxing that I fell asleep in the chair.

When she was done I woke up and was fascinated with the blending of the colors and how it made my features stand out. She even put on false eyelashes. I had never worn those before. They made my eyes stand out. When I was a little girl, starting at six years old, my mother sent me to a charm school where I was taught how to apply makeup. I used to wear it prior to my construction days. So I started buying makeup and now I wear it almost every day but it is for me, not any man who is or is not in my life.

A lot of men do not like women to wear makeup. It makes me smile, so I do it. I have had other similar situations where men assume that my behavior is about or for them. It tickles my funny bone. I, despite being a woman and a woman who loves men, do not focus my entire being on trying to impress men. The few women that I have met in life that do are miserable. What causes the misery is that every man is different. With each man they intend to impress, they are subject to have to make adjustments to their appearance and behavior. They are subject to the whim of the man they are with at this time. It is impossible to know every man's likes and dislikes. Heck, one man may like that outfit and the next man won't. It is critical to be pleasing to yourself. An added benefit to pleasing yourself is that you walk with confidence in it. You own the look. Confidence is the most attractive trait in both men and women. So do you boo!!! It will attract you (the one most compatible) to you.

Releasing the Pain

- *Acknowledging that it is over*

A common and major step necessary to preventing more devastating pain and releasing the pain I felt in my failed relationships has been to acknowledge that the relationship is over. Once I acknowledged that it was over, I began to behave as if the relationship is over. I had to accept that the relationship was not going to be for a lifetime. Sometimes it has been because I have discovered character traits that I find unacceptable. It may be that I have discovered a pattern of not keeping their word. There is nothing I can do to change that and it presents a problem of trust. If I can't trust what you tell me, then I am vulnerable to a lot of disappointment and hurt. Not a place I want to live.

Other times it has been due to life's circumstances. I met a man who was only separated from a woman he had been with for fifteen years. I did not know until about a month into the relationship that this was the case. I found out when he told me about her and the she had informed him that she was pregnant with, what would wind up being, their first child. I didn't know that he was merely separated or that she even existed during that first month because he entertained me at his apartment, cooking me a nice dinner and watching television, and I saw no signs that a woman had lived there. She had moved out, but when I questioned him further after he told me about her pregnancy, he told me that she had not taken all of her things.

Immediately, I knew that it meant she was not done with the relationship. Having had my own child, I knew that the woman likely, after fifteen years invested and carrying his child, would want to give the relationship another chance, if for no other reason than the child. In this case, I immediately ended the relationship on an intimate level. We remained friends, purely platonic friends. I helped him and his growing family find housing in the course of my employment. I never again crossed the line into a personal, intimate relationship with that man. There was no room for me in his life. I had to accept that and realize that although he was a lot of fun, he adored me, I adored him, he was not available to be in a relationship with me.

There are also times when I find that I simply am not compatible with the person's lifestyle or personality. I cannot date a drug dealer. Not because of some super high moral code. I am from the projects. I have no desire to look down on anyone. It is a more practical reason: I work too much with law enforcement and, even more importantly, I am responsible for a not-for-profit organization that is governed by the IRS code 501 c3. That subjects the organization to scrutiny. The hijackers involved in the 9/11 attacks on the United States laundered money through organizations with the same designation as our organization. It generated, rightfully so, much more scrutiny of the funds funneled through these types of organizations. There have been lots of organizations that have used that status to avoid paying taxes. The obvious conclusion when finding out that someone I had been dating briefly sold drugs,

I had to acknowledge that the relationship was not going to be suitable for me, and it was over.

In the last two examples, I was able to determine fairly quickly that the relationships would not work and had to end. There was very little pain involved. This is the best scenario, where you learn early that it is not a suitable relationship and end it *before* any pain sets in. At best, these situations caused disappointment.

The first circumstance, finding character traits that I am not prepared to live with, often takes a lot longer to surface. This is where the potential for pain is highest. On paper, if you will, the person looks like a great fit: physically attractive to me (because what I like may not be attractive to others), financially self-sufficient, kind, has a spiritual belief system and wants to be with me. Sounds great. However, it is only with the investment of time that character traits reveal themselves. They reveal themselves when a person is under stress, whether directly related to me or not. They reveal themselves when the person is in conflict with other people. They reveal themselves in a crisis. These all take time to see. Due to the investment of time, the relationship is producing fond memories. I am enjoying the companionship. Maybe it has even progressed to great sex by the time the character trait reveals itself.

I will stop here and say, briefly, that the longer I wait to engage in sex, the better the chances are that the character traits that are unacceptable will reveal themselves and the less chance there is that I miss them and the fact that they render the relationship unacceptable. The longer I wait to engage in sex, the more likely it is that I will *see* the character flaw. It's like the eye exam where squiggly lines appear on the screen and you are supposed to click the button when you see them. If you are paying very close attention, you see them. They appear and disappear very quickly. Just like the character flaws a person is willing to show at the beginning of a relationship. It sneaks out and they put it back really quick because they don't want you to see it. Once you are engaged in sex, your eyes are closed and your legs are open with your mouth moaning so you miss more than half the squiggly warning signs.

It takes objective focus to see the subtle, painless warning signs. Once we miss them, we proceed right onto the Hurt People Highway and pain. Still there are other times when a relationship has simply run its course. People grow and change. That is part of the very definition of life. The ability to change and grow. What I wanted in a relationship in my twenties and was willing to tolerate in a relationship in my twenties is very different than what I will have in a relationship today. The key here is that I have learned a lot of things about myself through the years that I have to incorporate into my choices. I know me now. This will be discussed further in the section on the "selection process."

When my partner looked at me when I came through the door with that unpleasant look on his face, somehow I knew the relationship was over. We did not fight or have a great big blow up, but the relationship was over. By acknowledging that to myself first, I was able to minimize the pain. It was not easy to let go because we had invested in each other. I knew that I had to end it before we caused damage to each other emotionally. Being willing to acknowledge the truth saved pain for both of us. He did not want to end the relationship, but in the long run, it was best for both of us that we did not continue in the relationship and begin to leave lasting scars in each other over time.

The most constructive thing to do when a relationship is at its end is to end it! Do not drag it out for months and even years, as I have seen people do. In dragging the relationship out you create the space to inflict pain on each other. Remember, you don't have to be mad to get out of a relationship. It is totally acceptable that it just end. If you realize that you no longer want to be with someone and you feel bad or think that ending it is going to hurt them and they don't deserve to be hurt, so you will just stay, realize that it is compassionate to be honest with them instead of staying and becoming resentful or disloyal and hurting them more deeply.

Whatever the reason the relationship has ended, acknowledging for myself that it is, in fact, time for it to end, has helped me to minimize the hurt and pain and release any pain that I feel. Addiction programs teach that the first step to overcoming an addiction is to first admit that there is a problem. This is the same principle. In fact, I can truly say that getting over the most painful relationship required me to treat it as an addiction.

After all, I realized that my addiction was a gorgeous, sexy, successful, spiritually-gifted MAN. There was no pill or drink that caused me to disregard my own needs or trample my dignity and pride. No, it was a fine ass MAN. I was addicted nonetheless. I had it bad. I wanted my addiction morning, noon and night. It was hard to kick the habit. A habit that, as I lived and learned a little more, I realized would never have allowed me to flourish and grow in my career or otherwise, not due to an attempt to control me or hold me back, but more because I had allowed his needs, lifestyle and everything else to dominate our life together.

It was all about him. There was very little consideration for my need to grow professionally. Looking back now, I don't see a path from that relationship to have been able to work in South Central Los Angeles helping my mother build the community. We would have been living more than an hour outside the city. When I began to work for my mother, I lived not far from him about 45 minutes outside the city. I recognized early that it was dangerous for me to drive that distance one way each day because in the stop-and-go traffic I was prone to doze off.

I quickly made the decision to move back into the city. In fact, I jokingly tell my son that we are probably the ONLY people to move back to South Central Los Angeles right after the riots. If I had still been in that relationship it is unlikely that I would have moved that far away from him. That single move changed the entire course of my life career-wise. It set me on a totally different path and I discovered two things that I love: construction and entertainment production.

The opportunity to discover these things about myself would not have surfaced in the kind of work I was doing. None of this would have been "his fault." It would have been my desire to keep things the way they were, despite the fact that this man never committed anything to me. He never adjusted his lifestyle to accommodate me. This was all my doing. I had the unhealthy relationship with myself and allowed him to have an unhealthy relationship with me. It is true that he brought his own unhealthy baggage to the relationship, but the biggest challenge for me was my own unhealthy baggage, not his. I would have willingly sacrificed my career for his. He was and is very successful. He always took great care of me financially. He provided well for me. In exchange, however, I would have had to give up being great in my own right. I would have had to dim my light and that is unacceptable.

• *Evaluating my participation*

I have discussed previously that the most painful day of my life was the day that I had to look myself in the mirror and admit that the excruciating pain I was experiencing was caused by my participation in the relationship. It was, in effect, my fault. The behavior that hurt so much was another person's, but it was as much my fault as his. How was it my fault that he decided to bring another woman in my face? How was it my fault that he continued to see me on Friday nights and bring her in my face on Sunday morning? How was it my fault that he broke promises to me so that he could be with her? How was it my fault that when I lay sick in his bed, he left to go have lunch with her? BECAUSE I ALLOWED IT. I

PARTICIPATED. There is no more simple truth than that. Remember, I had no example to draw from as a point of reference. I had never seen, in the day-to-day sense, how a couple was supposed to interact.

From the beginning of the relationship, when this man explained to me that he was not looking for a girlfriend, but that he wanted to spend time with me, I thought that I could handle that "situationship." I thought it would be all right as long as we were spending time together. I did not know that I could not spend all my free time with him, have incredible sex multiple times a week, go on vacations, spend lots of time exploring the spiritual laws of the universe (a huge part of our relationship and a huge turn on) and not develop deep feelings and want a committed relationship.

I went into the situation thinking I could handle it. It is like stepping into a river and it looks calm and shallow where you step in, only to go a few feet out and realize that it dropped off significantly and even worse, there is quicksand at the bottom. I was drawn in and had a heck of a time getting out. The harder I worked to prove myself worthy, the less he seemed willing to commit. When I would give up and try to walk away, he would pursue me to keep me there. We know that to get out of quicksand you can't fight too hard. I was fighting with everything I had to make him see that I was worthy and a good woman. The sad reality is that *he already knew that.* That was what attracted him in the first place. When he would criticize my hair, it would hurt my feelings and I would try to make it grow long, as he said he liked it that way. I did not know that if my hair being

105
Releasing the Pain

short was that big of a deal to him in the beginning, he never would have approached me in that way.

When he would complain about anything or start an argument about anything, it was to give himself justification to go be with another woman. I did not know that at the time. Almost all of this was shown to me after the relationship ended and I began to evaluate my participation in the drama. I allowed him to have me and other women. I allowed him to monopolize my time for "free." Free in the sense that he had no responsibility to me. In his mind, however, because he took care of any financial needs I had, he was doing all that was required.

He was several years older than me and I respected him on so many levels. I thought this arrangement -- the situationship -- I had agreed to was acceptable. I realize that I thought it would change over time. I don't remember it being a conscious thought, but looking back I honestly thought that after he saw what a good woman I was and he was a few years from his recent divorce, that he would want to commit to me and we would live happily ever after. I thought after I auditioned all of my talents I would win the day. After all, we had so much in common. We loved each other. That much I was certain of.

When I looked back on what I agreed to participate in, it was the ultimate source for all of the pain I experienced. I learned valuable lessons that have served me since that time. Understanding what I did and how it affected me allowed me to release the pain from it. I have never experienced that kind of pain over a failed relationship since that time. I put

Releasing the Pain

the knowledge I gained into practice. I do not agree to a non-committed arrangement with anyone that I think I might really want to be with. If I feel that I really could care about the person, I don't play with myself by telling myself I can accept less than what I want. Everything is based on what I am looking for in a relationship at that point in time. If I want a commitment, I don't accept less. If I just want to play, I play, but not with anyone that I believe has the potential to be a lifelong relationship.

Another very big lesson I learned from that experience was never to allow a man to exploit my insecurities in my physical appearance to control me. When he realized that I was sensitive about my hair and weight, he would use those things to criticize me and it would inflict intense pain. I would retreat and he would have freedom to be with other women. It was a conversation with my brother that changed this for me.

I talked to him about it one day. He asked me how much did I weigh when we met. I told him pretty much the same that I weighed that day. He explained to me that it seemed to him that the man was using it as an excuse to create distance. He further explained that the man clearly liked me the way that I was or he would never have been attracted to me. He suggested that I was what he actually liked, but that he may have been influenced by what society thought he should have.

He explained that if a man is not attracted to a woman, he doesn't approach her and he certainly doesn't spend years with her. Therefore, the complaints about my physical appearance were a

107
Releasing the Pain

smoke screen to give him cover for whatever he wanted to do. It taught me that whatever I look like the day a man meets and approaches me, is what he gets. He has no right to complain about my physical appearance as long as it does not drastically change from when he approached me. I believe that whatever he sees is what he signed up for. I believe that he has to accept me as I am, without changes, the same way I have to accept him the way he is, without changes.

If what I meet is not acceptable to me that day, then I should go find what it is that I am really looking for. If a man wants a woman 20 pounds lighter than me, then go find her. Don't try to change me; find what you're looking for. I am not second place or default material. I am the prize. Either you want this or you don't. This is me. Take it or leave it alone. Either way, I'm ok with me. I will not try to change you and not allow you to try to change me. It's just that simple. I don't subscribe to the notion that either party should have less than what they want. If I am not what you want, don't settle. Keep on moving down the road until you find what it is you want.

• *Forgiving myself*

For me, second only to acknowledging that I bore responsibility for the excruciating pain I suffered in a relationship, forgiving myself had to be the most significant step to releasing the pain of the relationship, the hardest thing to do and the best guarantee that I would never experience that kind of pain again. Forgiveness of anyone seems to be extremely difficult for people in general. The definition of forgive is: to cease to feel resentment against.

It's one thing to forgive another person, but to forgive myself was very hard. I kept thinking I should have known better. I didn't realize that the very reason I experienced the situation was to teach me the lesson. I expected myself to already know what I didn't know. I would not feel resentment toward a baby for not knowing how to spell cat. If the baby doesn't know, he or she just don't know. None of that stopped me from feeling resentment toward myself for allowing another person to control my emotions and heartstrings and hurt me so much. I am responsible for protecting my heart.

That is not the job of any man I meet. That is my job alone. It is my job to maintain the power that was given to me to make and keep me happy. The moment I turn that responsibility over to another human, I have lost. I have opened the door to pain. It is inevitable that I will experience pain when I am out of my rightful place and put someone in a place they are not supposed to inhabit. It is a recipe for disaster. In order to forgive myself, I had to understand *why* I allowed the imbalance of personal power to exist between the man and myself. It required me to evaluate *what I did* in the relationship as I discussed above.

Once I could see what I had done and recognize why I had done those things, I was able to forgive myself. It was difficult to admit that the reason I allowed my partner to get away with so many small disrespects was two-fold. The first reason was that, unconsciously, I did not believe that kind of man would stay with me because my father never made me feel that his love was permanent. He did not live with me and I always felt that access to his love was not guaranteed.

The second reason I allowed my partner to inflict so much pain was that I didn't have an example of what I could or should require from any partner. There were instincts that told me that the things I was being subjected to were not right, certainly not healthy, but I had no frame of reference to know what it *should* look like. It would be many years later before I consciously understood that I attracted the emotionally unavailable man whose emotional development had been stunted somewhere in his life and, further, required compassion and understanding of his inability to freely share their emotions.

It took years to understand that I had been taught that the plight of the man was my burden to bear. Well, I have learned to forgive myself for being uninformed. I wasn't mis-informed, I was simply un-informed. I had nothing, as the saying goes. All I had was desire for that man. He was the ideal man in my eyes. If I had to write on a piece of paper what I wanted the perfect man to be, his credentials, how he fit the bill. It was hard for me to admit that the relationship wasn't going to work. I blamed myself. I did not take into account his childhood, which was not pristine. His father was verbally, physically and emotionally abusive.

I recognize now that he did not have a great deal of respect for his mother. Those are two things that had absolutely nothing to do with me, but certainly affected our relationship. It affected his ability to freely love and commit to me. It was not that there was some deficiency in me that caused him to pull away at times. It was the result of his internal issues. You could never have convinced me of that then. I thought somehow I was not enough. It didn't matter that he told me on more than one occasion that I was too much woman for him. I didn't believe it. I had created an idol for myself in him. I worshipped the ground he walked on. After all, he was everything society said I should seek.

Again, he was my type. He was tall, dark, handsome, financially set, spiritually mature and shared my idea of how a household should function. I was ashamed that this relationship did not progress to marriage. I blamed myself. I did not realize that it probably did not matter what I did or did not do in that relationship, it was not the forever relationship. That man was placed in my life for a reason and a season. I am forever grateful for the relationship. I truly believe I became a woman in that relationship. I learned so many valuable lessons about relationships and even more about how universal spirit law operates.

I am no longer ashamed of the fact that the relationship didn't work. I understand that his personality needed to be the center of attention. I have always had an attention-gathering personality. Without trying. I can try to blend into a room and will inevitably be called into attention. It is who I am. As they say in today's slang, I woke up like this. It is not to my glory, but is for the purposes of the Creator that decided to show forth himself in all of us in different

Releasing the Pain

ways. I don't have any corner on that market. I am no more special than the next person. But I am special just as He created me and to the extent that He has developed me to this point. I will always be a work-in-progress because the Creator is infinite, but there are some things that he has fully matured in me and they are reflections of Him.

Once I matured in my understanding of spiritual things, I was able to forgive myself. Understanding that the hard experiences we go through are to teach us valuable lessons that are not just for us, but for us to share with others along the way. In fact, the most precious gifts we are endowed with are not for us, but for us to serve others with. The same compassion and understanding that I was willing to give to my father and the men in my life for their emotional under-development, I had to give to myself. I had to forgive myself for not knowing that I deserved to be cherished and committed to. I deserved and had a right to demand that any man that wanted access to my talents, gifts and time had to be responsible to me to have access. If he didn't want to be responsible to me, then he could not have access to me.

I also would no longer allow a man to pick and choose the parts of me that he wanted to have without responsibility for all of me unless it was mutually agreeable. What does that mean exactly? Well, if a man enjoys having conversations with me about business, he can't occupy all of my time and all we do is discuss his or my business ideas. This is important because I know that if I allow a man to occupy all of my time, he is in the space that my husband should be occupying.

I cannot spend all of my free time with a man who is not my husband if I ever expect to have a husband. Men sense the presence of another man. No matter what we *say* about the nature of our relationship, a man senses when a woman is available for a relationship. On the other hand, if I enjoy talking to a man about business, I will engage in that with him, but his access to me will be limited because he will have no responsibility toward me. The most precious amounts of my time and, certainly, my body, are reserved for the man who wants to accept all of me and be responsible for and to me.

Through the years, I have engaged in many kinds of relationships. The difference has been that I am conscious of what I am signing up for and only sign up for what I want to engage in. Once involved, if it is no longer satisfying to me, I exit. It keeps things simple. I take full responsibility for my own happiness prior to getting into a relationship. I am not looking for anyone to "complete me." I know that I am complete in a room alone and all by myself. The key is for me to engage with men who are also complete. I am not a nursemaid for a man's emotional body. There is no amount of changing *me* that is going to fix *his* internal issues.

For example, I could never stop communicating with enough men to make a jealous man feel secure in our relationship. That is an emotional issue that only he can fix. I am responsible to ensure that I don't participate in relationships that I know are subject to cause me pain. I know, for me, that I don't do well in an un-defined, no-labels-type relationship.

People often say they don't see why they have to put a label on their relationship. I say, you don't. But remember, anything that is not defined is NOTHING. Without a definition, there is no "relationship." There may be a "situationship," but not a "relationship." It is extremely dangerous emotionally to give another person access to your gifts, talents, time, money, human resources, home, family, body and so much more without a clear understanding of the requirements for continued access.

The danger for me was in giving too much and getting too little in return. But it was my fault because I didn't require the accountability. If I want to drive a Rolls Royce, I have to buy it. I don't get to buy just the symbol and then claim I own a Rolls Royce. I have to take responsibility for the entire car: the cost of acquiring it, the cost of maintenance and repairs, the cost of insurance and providing a place for it to be stored, like a garage or driveway.

If I am not willing to accept responsibility for all of those things, I am not qualified to own a Rolls Royce. Period. Well, I am as high quality as a Rolls Royce so why would I allow someone access to just the symbol without keeping me maintained, insured and in a suitable place? I had to forgive myself for allowing this in the past. It has saved me from so much pain.

Another reason I don't do well in relationships that have a loose definition or no label is that I don't know what I should expect or, more importantly,

Releasing the Pain

how I should behave in the relationship. If I am in a dating relationship that is not exclusive, I know that all we can do is spend time together. I do not expect this man to be there for me when I want him to be. He may not be available all the time. Neither should I be available every time he calls either. That is a fair exchange. If I ever choose to have a purely sexual relationship, and I have made this choice (I don't want to give the impression that I am above a purely sexual relationship), then the sex is a rare occurrence and that is all that I do with that person.

He has to make the sex an experience, though. It means that I am not involved with anyone else sexually and don't envision a long-term, committed relationship with this man. I won't have sex too frequently. I do not believe it is possible to engage in sex regularly with anyone and not become emotionally attached. Either the man or the woman is going to become emotionally attached. I strongly believe it is because sex is the most intimate activity we can engage in with another person. We can't share that with anyone regularly without developing an emotional attachment. I firmly believe that two consenting adults can consent to whatever type of relationship that they want. I do not want anyone to mistake my position. However, I know that whatever the nature of the relationship is it needs to be clearly defined and agreed to by both parties or it is likely to lead to misunderstanding and hurt.

I am just not into hurt. I need to know what to expect and what is expected of me. If my need for that amount of clarity is too much for a man, then he is not suitable to have access to my time, gifts or talents. I have had to forgive myself my previous ignorance and behavior that is likely to lead me to hurt and pain. Anything that I learn is a blessing.

• *Learning the lessons*

The process of evaluating a failed relationship and, particularly, my part that contributed to the failure, has proven to be invaluable. I always learn something more about me. I focus heavily on me because that is the only thing I have any hope of changing or controlling. I am wise enough now to know that I cannot change another person.

The man that I meet is the man that I would be in relationship with. It is unfair and unrealistic to think that a grown man is going to miraculously change his style, habits or character. The character is the area that is most important for me to evaluate early in a relationship. I see the character as the core of the man. This is what will drive all behavior. Character flaws are always a big deal to me because I recognize that these are things that have little chance of changing. We are who we are. I choose to believe a person when they show me who they are. Habits, on the other hand, are less etched in stone and may be tolerated. We all have habits that are annoying to other people. I put these in the "nobody's perfect" category. I have habits people find annoying. If I can adjust them while in that person's presence, I try to do so. It is my attempt at compromise and being less annoying to someone that I want to spend time with.

Style is a tricky one. It is often rooted in a person's self-image. It is often something that is a reflection of how they see themselves and not subject to change either. If I don't like a man's style, his choice of fashion, I expect that that is not subject to change. There are some people who found a style they liked in the 80's or 90's and will not wear up-to-date fashions. This is hard to break them from. Suggesting a makeover can merely be a suggestion. If they are willing, great. If they are not, you have to decide whether you want to be seen with them in those biker shorts at every picnic.

In evaluating a failed relationship, I have been able to learn lessons that prevent me from making the same mistakes over and over again. This requires me to spend a little time *between* relationships alone so that I have the mental space to learn the lessons. For me, at the time of a breakup, there is always some emotional discomfort at the very least. At its worst, there is emotional devastation. It has taken some time for me to be ready to evaluate my role and see the lessons I need to learn. If I jump right into another full-on relationship, I have not allowed myself time to see the lessons and will likely make the same mistake in the current relationship that I made in the last one. I suspect the results will be the same. In order to identify and grasp the lessons that I needed to learn, I had to spend time alone being honest about my behavior. Did I give too much? Did I require too little? Was I moving too fast? Did I engage in sex too soon? What caused me pain? How did I allow those things to occur?

If you notice, none of those questions are about what "he" did. They are all about what "I" did. This, again, is the only area that I believe I stand any

Releasing the Pain

chance of correcting. I am getting up in age and can't see in the dark as well as I used to. It is not the dark that can or will have to change in order for me to function in that room. If I want to find something in the dark room, I have to turn on the light now.

I just accepted that reality and changed my behavior. Once I realized that I was spending so much time being frustrated looking for my slipper under the bed in the dark when if I simply turned on the light I would have found it much sooner, it was not a big deal and I did not beat myself up about the need to change my behavior. Changing my behavior in relationships was just as simple, but because it involved my heart and emotions, I found it more difficult to accept.

Many people spend all of their energy focusing on the other person's behavior. I find that looking outward has never helped me find out how to correct my situation. I know people that never do anything wrong, if you listen to them. It is always someone else's fault that they have not had the success that they feel they deserve in relationships or anything else in life. The reality is that as long as you are pointing your finger at another person and not addressing the three fingers pointing back in your direction, you will never learn the lessons that will free you from failure.

This applies in every area of our lives. The lessons to prevent us from experiencing future pain are always in the three fingers pointing back at us. Always. Until we acknowledge our part in our failures, there is no way for us to achieve success. We have to understand what we did that worked against

Releasing the Pain

our success. Success is defined differently for each person, so looking at my success will not always give you the answers to success for you.

There is one ingredient necessary for any success in any area: work. Yes, you have to work at anything to be successful. Especially relationships of the heart. It is not enough to be there. There must be constant tending to a relationship. If you think of a relationship as a muscle, it has to have continual activity to remain fit. It is only when it is neglected that it becomes flabby and out of condition.

Once that happens, it is difficult for the muscle to function and seems twice as hard to get it back in shape. A relationship that has been allowed to get flabby is twice as hard to return to its glory days. Whatever you do to get into a relationship you must continue to do in order for that relationship to last. No person is going to be exactly what you want every day. We are human. Relationships, like people, evolve.

It is critical, however, not to allow intimate relationships to devolve into merely transactional arrangements. I have heard cynical, disillusioned people say that marriage is simply an arrangement. Their marriage was merely an arrangement because they did not tend to the emotional needs of each other throughout the relationship. They stopped communicating unless it was about finances.

Men are hunters and providers. They often express their love through provisions for a woman and children. They are dismayed to find out that the woman doesn't *feel* loved. They are perplexed as to why she doesn't know that he loves her. He is showing her the way he knows how. She needs something more; She needs his heart.

Similarly, if a woman thinks that her only role is to provide sex and food, she is perplexed as to why he is unsatisfied. He needs her appreciation and support for his efforts. If she thinks he is supposed to provide and therefore doesn't need to be appreciated or respected for doing so, she is failing to give him what he needs. Each of these relationship mistakes are due to laziness. They stem from the idea of what the other person is supposed to be doing and not focusing on the work necessary to keep the relationship alive and thriving.

Personally, I want a thriving relationship. If it isn't that, never mind. There is too much work and compromise involved in sharing space with and being responsible for and to another person to do that with someone just for the sake of doing it. Resentment begins to set in when people are only in a relationship for convenience or appearance. I know too many people who did this for years, only for the relationships to end in disaster anyway. The parties come out of the relationship scarred and battered. Some come out bitter and never recover.

We can release all of the pain from these experiences by acknowledging that, yes, we became comfortable and only looked at the relationship as a convenience, rather than something that needed to be tended to regularly. We did not treat the relationship as something that required work constantly to thrive and further required us to meet the emotional needs of the other person,

Instead, we dismissed their needs, outside of transactions, as drama or an attempt to manipulate and control. This becomes habitual and will carry from relationship to relationship if we never stop and acknowledge our own stuff. If we never call it like it is. The pain will build on top of the pain of the last failed relationship and we will become bitter. We never learn the lessons and therefore, are doomed to repeat the cycle until we learn the lessons.

Usually in those relationships that were never intended to last a lifetime, the reason for the relationship is to teach us valuable lessons that we must learn in order to be suitable for the lifetime relationship. If we despise the learning, we doom ourselves to a cycle of failure. Learn the lessons, accept that you are not perfect and don't know everything so that you can experience a thriving relationship.

- *Putting the lessons learned from previous relationships into practice in every future relationship.*

With all of the pain associated with learning the lessons of a failed relationship, I am astonished when I talk to people during their learning process and then see them fail to put the information into practice in the next relationship. If I learned from the most recent relationship that allowing a man to monopolize my time without a commitment to me sets me up for hurt, the next time a man tries to do, the appropriate response is to call it out and if the man doesn't want to make any adjustments thank him and send him on his way.

This may be why we act as if we didn't *just* go through this and learned that it didn't work. Once we *know*, we are *responsible* for what we know. It may require us to walk away from a new situation that, on the surface, seemed to hold so much promise. Once we get something in our sights, we would rather make excuses for bad behavior than to walk away. Walking away seems so final. Often, however, it is not final. It merely gives enough separation for each person to realize that they really want to invest the time and energy to have the relationship. Our mistake is in putting the lessons learned from the previous failures into practice.

As I discussed previously, I realized that, for me, it is not good for me to allow a man to have access to all of my time and talents without being committed to me. I don't know how to function in that arena without getting hurt. So any man who comes along with that as a proposition doesn't get past first base with me. It is not that he is a bad person. He is just not the person for me. I can't tie myself up with someone and allow them to fill the space that the right person should be in because, when and if, the right person comes along, they will keep moving because they see that someone else is already in that spot. A man who is serious about being a partner to a woman will not engage with a woman who already has someone, or even some-thing, in that space. I added some-thing because it could be a career, her children, her extended family or volunteer work that occupies too much space in her life that he doesn't see room for him and will keep moving.

I am curious how many men did not pursue a woman because they perceived that there were things that she would not be willing to give up to make room for him in her life. You will be tested on the lessons learned in previous relationships. I distinctly remember being tested after I learned that it is asking for hurt, disappointment and pain to get involved with a man that is already involved with someone else, especially a married man.

In fact, I have learned that it doesn't matter if he is married or not. The fact that he is involved with someone else is enough to cause the same level of disappointment, hurt and pain. Once I learned this lesson about myself, I think I must have grown a sign on my backside saying: test her, she swears she isn't fooling with married men. It seemed to me that every married or hooked-up man in the world wanted to have me as his side-piece. I was beating them away with a stick. Eventually they stopped approaching me. This was the case because in anything, if we say we have learned a lesson we will be tested on it. There is a reason that in order to graduate from one grade to the next or even one part of a curriculum to the next, you have to take a test. The instructor or institution wants to know that you fully grasped the lessons they just taught you before they can attest to your fitness for the next level.

A lot of people perceive the tests as negative and don't test well. They may know the information, but don't like the testing process. Well, in relationships, we will be tested on what we say we have learned. We will be confronted with the same thing over and over until we prove that we have learned and are applying the previous lessons. If we don't despise the test-taking, we can achieve the highest degree of satisfaction in relationships. I don't care what people say, how many times they profess they have sworn off love, declared that love doesn't exist, everyone is imbued to want a loving relationship. Just watch them when they meet someone that they think might be "the one." You will see how fast they change their cyclical story. Those who don't, are simply miserable.

Chapter

IDENTIFYING THE ELEMENTS

Every relationship is different because no two people are exactly the same. We were created different. It makes life interesting. Variety is the spice of life. However, the way to avoid hurt and pain is pretty consistent. There are elements of a healthy relationship and there are elements of an unhealthy relationship. Being able to identify which is which is critical knowledge to have.

The simple way to know if the relationship is healthy or unhealthy is to have a clear definition. I was trained in my metaphysical training at the Institute of Divine Metaphysical Research of Pasadena how to investigate the true nature of things and one of the principle tools we used was the dictionary. It is available to everyone. There was no particular one so that the institute could not claim ownership of the words we defined.

In other words, definitions are universal. The reason for using the dictionary was to learn the actual meaning of words and sometimes the etymology of the words -- the roots of the words. Often, people have an idea what the word means or we generally accept a definition because it is how it is used in language daily. However, upon looking up the definition you may find that what you thought it means is not the only definition of the word, despite its common acceptance as the definition.

With this training as a tool that has been ingrained in my soul, I spent years studying three days a week, whenever I have been asked or motivated to research something, I go to the dictionary to get the meaning of the words of the topic.

In 2003, a friend and colleague, Dr. Meschellia Johnson, was planning a conference for women. She has spent a significant part of her career focusing on the needs of women and young girls. She was planning a conference and asked me to do a workshop on "healthy relationships."

I agreed and, as I had been trained, started at the beginning by looking up the definition of each word. It gave me a great vehicle to identify the elements in a healthy relationship and present them to the women at the conference. I did not know then, that Dr. Johnson considered me "the relationship lady."

It would be many years later, as I talked to her about facilitating a group every week with men on relationships that she said just that. She said, "You have always been the relationship lady." I was shocked a little, but she reminded me that we used to stay after work and talk about relationships. I had forgotten how much time we spent discussing relationships. She reminded me that I had always given her the best advice about relationships.

It brought me back to 2003 when she asked me to do the workshop on healthy relationships. I have used that presentation over and over again. The research I did holds true no matter who is involved in the relationship or the nature of the relationship. Here is the definition of both words as defined by Webster's:

Healthy: 1) Enjoying health; 2) conducive to health; 3) (synonyms) **Wholesome - implies appearance and behavior indicating soundness and balance.** *(This definition is most readily applicable to relationships)*

Relationship: 1) the state of being related or interrelated; 2) the relation connecting or binding participants in a relationship;
3) ***a state of affairs existing between those having relations or dealings.*** *(This definition gives a clear picture of the behavior, which is what we need to identify.)*

Combined, a healthy relationship is: ***Appearance and behavior indicating soundness and balance in a state of affairs existing between those having relations or dealings***

Having words to describe exactly what a healthy relationship is gives us a common language so that when we get into the conversation, we are not discussing what we "think" a healthy relationship is, but rather, what it is. Having a clear definition gives us a foundation to start with that is not subjective, but objective. My definition, or opinion, of a healthy relationship is no more valid than your definition/opinion. We could go on indefinitely about our opinion on what is healthy and what is not in a relationship. That won't fix any real problems. Once we come to an agreement on the terms, we can proceed with a constructive conversation. For me, the best way to remove opinion and supposition is to get the actual meaning. It is not subjective when we use actual definitions. Exploring the definition:

The first part of the definition is what is healthy. This applies to physical and emotionally healthy things. Let's apply the definition to food for a minute. The food, in order to meet the definition, has to have the appearance and behavior indicating soundness and balance. It is where the term "balanced diet" is derived, I'm sure.

If we eat a diet of primarily fast foods, sodas, chips, cookies and sweets, we will cause our bodies to become addicted to the sugars and fats and bring on diabetes, hypertension, heart disease and possibly even death. No one would argue that the diet described above is balanced. The imbalance in the diet causes disease and poor health. It is not sound behavior to feed our bodies this way and expect them to function normally.

While we may, in appearance, be feeding our bodies, the behavior is depriving our bodies of actual nutrients because we are not providing enough fruits and vegetables to nourish the cells and not enough water to keep us hydrated. So the appearance that we are nourishing our bodies is there, but the behavior is not. In order to be healthy, we have to have both the appearance and behavior indicating soundness of food choice and balance in the type of foods we eat.

I can't imagine anyone arguing with a doctor that a diet of processed junk foods and fast foods is what is best for their body physically. Even in cases where people are morbidly obese, they don't argue with the doctor that it is healthy for them. They usually describe how hard it is to stop eating the things that make them unhealthy, but not that it IS healthy to eat that way. Why, then, when we engage in an unhealthy relationship do we argue with ourselves that the relationship is worth saving? We should stay in an unbalanced, shaky relationship. Is it because we are more concerned about the *appearance* than the *behavior*?

Many times, people do not want to be alone and give the appearance that they are somehow incapable of having a relationship. I know women who, if they have not seen me in a while, ask me: Do you have a man? It's as if the only thing that validates my existence is the presence of a man. I am clear that it is not good for man to be alone, or woman for that matter, which is why the Creator created the woman. However, if I, as a woman, am not healthy enough to *be with me*, then how would I expect any other person to *be with me* and it produce a healthy relationship?

If we relate a relationship to our diet, it may give us a way to examine the relationship from the beginning to prevent us from entering unhealthy relationship after unhealthy relationship. When we examine our history, we will see that we have a history with the same type of person. This leads to the same results.

The reason is simple. We keep feeding our cravings. We start off with the same elements. We start with the same junk foundation. My particular brand of relationship junk food was emotionally unavailable men needing someone to be empathetic to their plight, at the expense of my needs and feelings. Junk food, for sure. Heck, it feels good to help someone. No one can argue with that, right? Well I can, now. I know better. I began to add concerned about my needs, feelings, desires and wants as behavior that must be present to my man-diet. It caused me to lose some man-weight too. What? Yes. The man who is so broken that he needs a life-line no longer approaches me.

I must have developed a repellent that keeps them from even coming my way. I have spent a lot of time alone, but I have been able to use that time to develop a healthy, sound relationship with myself, which is the most important relationship I have. We will discuss the first relationship in another chapter. I lost the dead weight of a dependent and added the good fats and carbs for energy. Men now have to add energy to the relationship. They cannot be simply a drain and a lot of calories. I figure, with all of the work involved in maintaining the relationship muscle, I might-as-well have someone who is going to invigorate the heck out of me. He sure as heck should be easing my weight and responsibility.

I have men in my life who simply make my life easier. They are not lovers, but they certainly do everything within their power to make my life easier. The mere fact that I have been able to attract more than one man who takes responsibility for relieving my burdens is proof that I have made the appropriate shift in my man-diet.

These men love me and have said as much. We are not, nor have we ever been, lovers. It is not necessary to be sexually involved in order to love and show love for each other. It does not hurt that they are all very handsome. That, however, is not the attraction that we feel toward each other. Be clear, I give as good as I get in these relationships, even to the women in their lives, if it helps them.

Our relationships are sound and balanced in their appearance but most importantly in behavior. I do not cross the line with these men. In fact, all of them, except one, have spouses or significant others in their lives. I am careful not to infringe on that relationship through my behavior. I recognize and respect appropriate boundaries. These men are not in an intimate, personal, sexual relationship with me. Therefore, I do not call them after a certain hour at night. I do not ask them to do things with me that are strictly personal, like go to the movies or dinner unless there is a special occasion or reason. I do not entertain them in my home alone. These men function more like brothers to me. They treat me like a queen. They will go out of their way to lighten my load. I love and appreciate them for that. However, we have boundaries and we stay within those boundaries to ensure that the relationships remain healthy for everyone. I maintain a healthy man-calorie-count with them.

The most important thing to take away from this section is to recognize that there are elements that are healthy and there are unhealthy elements in relationships. At the beginning of a relationship, instead of focusing on physical junk food -- yes honey, sex and how cute he is -- we need to be building healthy bones in our behavior that will sustain the relationship. We always want to rush to the dessert before we eat the vegetables. Guilty as charged. Now, I have a handle on my man-sweet-tooth. I can wait. I don't care how good it appears, if it is not sound and balanced in behavior, I can wait for the next train.

Another one of my mother's sayings was: You don't have to be a ballerina and dance on every stage. I don't have to dance with every man that shows up in my life. Certainly there isn't enough room on my dance card to dance with all of them just because they came to the dance. I don't want anyone to think this only applies to women. The same rules apply to men. While men do have some capacity to engage in sexual activity simply for the physical release and not get emotionally entangled, there is only "some" capacity.

Men lose perspective once they engage in sexual activity early in a relationship as well. They miss the early warning signs. The longer they wait to engage in sexual activity and spend time on getting to know the character and personality of a woman, the more likely they will avoid the monster-in-cute-form.

At the beginning of the relationship is where the effort to get to see the person is crucial. This is the time when you will be able to clearly see the character flaws, the personality quirks and anything else that can potentially derail the relationship. However, you need objective vision to see these things. Objective

Identifying the Elements

vision is distracted, if not totally clouded, when sex is involved.

• *What does unhealthy look like?*

When a relationship is unhealthy, usually the people involved are the last to know. It is always clearer to family and friends because they are not intimately, or closely, involved and have a more objective vantage point. This is not to suggest that it is impossible to see the signs if you are intimately involved with someone. Often, family and friends know your relationship history. They remember how devastated you were the last time.

Friends and family saw signs that the person was controlling early on. They noticed the things that you simply wrote off as a little too much, but so cute. The jealous mate is a good example of this. When the relationship is new, you find it cute that the person shows a little jealousy. It makes you feel that they are really into you.

Well, family and friends see the crazy that is underneath that. They don't find it cute. They recognize the little ways that the person finds to keep you from getting together now. They notice that you always hurry off the phone when the person comes in the room. There are a million little signs that the jealousy is an issue.

Due to our involvement in the relationship and our desire for it to work, we will often overlook the warning signs. Hopefully, we can become more astute at seeing them and responding appropriately at the beginning. Warning signs do not have to be the end of the relationship. They can simply be things that need to be communicated and understood. If we see early that the moment you get a phone call from someone, your new mate/friend has to find a reason to distract you from the call, that is when you should bring it to their attention and explain that it is inconsiderate and is likely to cause a problem in the relationship.

If the behavior continues it tells you that one of two things is true: they can't help it; or they don't want to stop. For your purposes, it doesn't matter whether they can't or won't, they do not stop the behavior.

Now you have only two choices: stay or leave. If you stay, you must expect the behavior to continue and more than likely get worse. People are on their best behavior at the beginning. At the beginning everyone wants to put their best foot forward. Once we have been involved for a while, we become more comfortable and let down the guardrails to our particular brand of crazy.

If you stay in a relationship after you have identified habits or character flaws, the choice is yours and you have to own it. You have essentially said that you will accept this behavior in the future. Everyone has the right to choose the flaws and habits that they will deal with. This is not for others to decide. The only person who can tell you what works for you is you. Again, you own all of it though. You can't blame the person you are in relationship with once you know the flaw exists. Since we all have flaws, we should be willing to accept some flaws in the other person. I love the saying: He is not perfect, but he's perfect for me.

Most of us continue to attract to us and be attracted to the person that allows us to be who we are. This is true because the law of attraction brings to us what we are or what we focus on most heavily. Also, we like what we like. If we are givers, we tend to attract takers we can give to. If we are outdoor-types, we are attracted to outdoor-types. Whatever our "thing" is, we tend to attract and be attracted to the same type over and over again.

If we take the time after a failed relationship to evaluate our participation, as strongly suggested earlier, we will see where the offensive behavior took root in the relationship. We will be able to see what you participated in that led to so much hurt and pain. We will be able to see the similarity in traits in all of your relationships. The hard part is to acknowledge them and act accordingly.

Usually, the appropriate thing to do is not what we want to do. Usually it is appropriate to end the relationship and that is not what we want. We want what we want, without the parts we don't want. Oh, if he would just not -- you fill in the blank -- he would be perfect. If she only- - fill in the blank -- I would marry her.

Whatever our brand or thing is, we continue to see it in our past relationships if we simply take the time to look. Having done this exercise, I noticed my pattern of behavior that revealed my unhealthy habits. I did not require balance in the giving in my relationships. I gave without requiring that I receive the same or similar consideration.

If the man had a justifiable reason for being self-centered, I factored that in and it didn't matter how it affected my feelings, needs or wants. I just accepted it. Not anymore. When I see that a man is enjoying the benefits of me but I do not receive what I need, that is a huge warning sign for me that I am starting off the wrong way and I have to correct course or end the relationship because it is certainly going to lead to hurt and pain. I refuse to go too far on that Hurt People Highway because it has familiar landmarks that I have seen before. They may have put a new coat of paint on that building, but it is the same one I went into the last time. I think I'll just skip the tour this time.

For me, the key is to identify early if there are things that I know are likely to lead to pain for me. It does not matter if other people think he should have a better job, drive a nicer car or wear a different style of clothes. Those things don't matter to me. If I like his style, car and he can financially handle what I need him to handle, I don't care about anyone else's opinion on those things.

Where I SHOULD be paying attention to the opinion of family and friends is when they point out things that could be harmful to me. I always try to listen to the opinions of those close to me. I am very careful, however, not to discuss my relationship with people who are negative about everything or those people who I know secretly hope that my relationship fails.

Yes, there are people close to you that secretly hope your relationships fails. You know who they are if you think about it. Those people that I trust, I listen to their concerns even if I don't readily agree with their assessment. I try to surround myself with people who still believe that it is possible to have a great relationship. The jaded, scorned, miserable haters? I don't discuss my relationship with them. I am not interested in their negative view of the world. I have friends who are married and work hard every day to make their marriages thrive. Those are the people who I lean on for input, vision and encouragement.

The fact that we like what we like, we attract what we are and we have a "type" all make it easy for us to engage in the same relationship over and over. Fortunately or unfortunately, we get the same result over and over. This means that the same unhealthy behaviors are likely to follow us from one relationship to the next.

The way to break this cycle is through evaluating our behavior. When we have identified our pattern, we will see familiar behavior in the person we have started a relationship with and in ourselves that are a clear giveaway that we are headed the same way on that same old road. It requires honesty with ourselves. We have to be willing to admit and own our own stuff. As stated previously, as long as we look outwardly at the behavior of the other person, we will never be able to identify the solution. We have to see the solution in us. Once we have identified old behavior or see old behavior in the new person, we must -- that did not say should, it said must -- respond appropriately by either changing our behavior immediately or requiring the other person to change the behavior we identified.

I am not saying we can change the other person. It requires a conversation to set the requirement, establish the boundary. Once that conversation is held, we have to watch for behavior change in the other person. We do not need to repeat the requirement every chance we get. The change in the other person, just as with you, will only happen if he or she chooses to make the change. Some behavior patterns are so ingrained in a person that it has become second nature. In order for that to change, the person has to make a concerted effort. It has to be a conscious choice to change. It does not require them to be perfect at it immediately, but the effort has to be apparent. Otherwise, it takes me back to the fact that they either can't or won't change the behavior.

For your purposes, it doesn't matter which. The behavior does not change. You have to either accept the behavior and stay or, recognize the potential for hurt and pain is too great and leave. There is no gray area. It is not complicated. Even if you have children together. Yes, even if you have children. The best thing you can do for your children is to expose them to healthy relationships and how to appropriately respond when they are involved in unhealthy ones.

This chapter is to help identify what is unhealthy so that it can be avoided. There is too much dysfunction in our communities. All communities. It is not confined to one race, socio-economic group, men or women, gay/lesbian, straight or any other group. Relationship dysfunction is rampant world-wide. It is the reason that we have so much conflict. People bring to every new relationship every past relationship. The dysfunction that we have begun to accept as "just the way it is" does not *have* to be the way it is.

If we all begin to turn within and correct our own dysfunction first, we will bring a healthier person to a new relationship. Start with self. On the airplane, they advise you before you ever take off the ground, if the cabin loses pressure and the oxygen mask that will provide oxygen comes out, put your own mask on BEFORE assisting others.

You can't help someone if you are passed out from lack of oxygen! This is why I continue to assert that you must look at your own behavior for the problem and solution before you look at others. It does not mean that other people are not at fault or responsible for their behavior and any hurt and pain they cause. They must face that. They are responsible to clean up their dysfunction. When individuals are healthy and come together in relationship, the result is a healthy relationship. If everyone would get healthy, families would be healthy, neighborhoods would be healthy, cities would be healthy and so on. If the ingredients are healthy, the dish is healthy. The opposite is also true. We see evidence of this every day.

• *Unhealthy elements*

There are behavior patterns and elements in a relationship that are unhealthy. When we see them, we must address them immediately, especially when it is our behavior. When we see it in others, we have to set requirements and/or boundaries. How do you know the relationship is unhealthy? We can determine this from the definition of healthy. Any behavior that is not rooted in soundness (truth) and balance (reciprocity) is likely unhealthy. Some simple tests to identify unhealthy patterns are:

- When the relationship frequently causes either party pain
- When there is disrespect between the parties
- When it is dominated by one party's issues, needs, wants, desires, personality
- When either party is controlled by fear
- When there's "always something" – as in… drama
- When its not FUN

In general, if any of these things describe the nature of your relationship, it is unhealthy. Something needs to change. Over many years, the last one has become my go-to evaluation tool. It is simple for me to understand and evaluate. If I am not having fun, it is time for me to make adjustments or stop doing whatever it is I'm doing. Like the time I went skiing with a group of friends in Mammoth. It was bitter cold outside. We decided to take lessons.

The class was probably too large, so it meant that we wound up standing still in the cold for a long time before we got to try the techniques. There was a lady in the perfect pink snowsuit. She was matching from head to toe. All she kept saying every few minutes was: I got on $500 worth of ski clothes and all I want to know is, are we having fun yet. It was the funniest part of the lesson. I still don't know how to ski, but I do know to ask myself if I'm having fun yet.

Identifying the Elements

I know people who have to have drama. They do not know how to function in a situation where everything is going well. They know how to defend themselves. They know how to manipulate. They don't know how to be loved, cherished and appreciated. I have seen men and women sabotage a potentially good relationship because they were unhealthy and did not know how to receive the genuine, healthy, loving behavior being shown them. One lady I know had about a two-week window. Things in her relationship would be going really well. Her and the guy were enjoying each other's company, laughing often, great sex and the world was right.

At about the two-week mark, she would pick a fight. She was more comfortable in dealing with pain and crisis and less comfortable with simply loving and enjoying so she created the atmosphere she was used to. The sad thing is that the two people were really good together when it was good. They just couldn't maintain it because she had to have drama.

Some people are hurt in childhood and learn to protect themselves by putting up a hard exterior. If someone breaks through that barrier, it makes them extremely uncomfortable. They have to push the person out of *that* space and into their comfort zone. Just remember, nobody has ever accomplished anything great from their "comfort zone." You can't have the relationship you always wanted without making yourself vulnerable to great love and, yes, pain. Let's look a little closer at unhealthy elements.

- *Built on a faulty foundation (lies, deception, need vs. want)*

Whatever ingredients you put into the relationship are going to be what comes out of it. Another of my mother's sayings: You can't squeeze lemon juice out of a rock. No lemon, no lemon juice. What couples build the relationship on is its foundation and will always be what it stands on. People evolve and grow over time, so cracks in a foundation can be fixed, but the sooner they are fixed the easier it is to fix them. The longer they go unaddressed, the harder it is to fix them. The more work it will require.

As a construction manager, I can tell you that if you pour the concrete foundation of your building and notice that as it cures it forms cracks, if you chip out that portion of the foundation before you move forward, as costly as it may be at the time, the cost to tear down the building or the lawsuits from the building collapsing are much greater than if you fix it as soon as it is identified. This principle can be used in building the foundation of a relationship. It is less costly in two ways if the cracks are fixed early. It will require less work to repair the problem and there will be less pain to overcome.

The foundation of a healthy relationship cannot be lies or deception. I don't ask anyone to take my word for this. All you have to do is look at the relationships where one person comes into the relationship cheating on his or her current mate.

The new person finds out later that the person is in another relationship. The trust, a necessary building block for any relationship foundation, is splintered and almost impossible to repair. As a woman, in the days when I would even consider dating a man who had another woman, I wanted to be given the opportunity to make my own choice to participate.

Lying to me made me feel like you thought I was stupid. That was more hurtful than the fact that you would never be mine. You thought I was so stupid I would never discover that you had another woman. You thought I would always be satisfied with the crumbs you were able to steal away from the other relationship.

That was an insult to my intelligence. Not a good thing for me. Being the youngest of six, it was not in me to allow anyone to think I couldn't keep up mentally. I had to learn how to keep up with five other people to get along and get what I needed in my household. I prided myself on my mental abilities. I survived five siblings. If you have siblings, you know what a big deal this is.

If the relationship is not built on trust, respect and truth there is no way that it will withstand the pressures that every relationship will face. Recently a friend of mine met a man at an event. This was not a club event, but an event at a restaurant. The man told her that he had been watching her all night and wanted to know if he could escort her to her car. She allowed him to since it was very close, there were lots of other people around and he seemed nice.

This man gave her a fake last name. Ultimately she found out that he was married and a preacher. How did he expect to build anything on that foundation of lies and disrespect for not only her, but his wife and most importantly himself? He lied about his name. It doesn't get more basic than that. He clearly had no intention of having a relationship, but rather was looking for a situationship. He did not care that it would hurt her that he had deceived her. It clearly did not occur to him that she could have been so hurt as to attempt to hurt him or his wife. His entire family could have been hurt. She could have simply showed up at his church and made a scene. Everything he had could have been in danger because he lied and tried to engage a woman in a relationship that he was not available to be in.

If a young woman goes to a nightclub using fake identification and meets a man who she lies to about her age, how does she expect him to trust her about anything in the future? There is no way to trust someone who lies to you about the most basic things. Your name, age, marital or relationship status, where you live, what you do for a living are all in the basic category.

So if you lie to someone about any of these things or someone lies to you about them, the relationship is doomed to fail because it started off wrong. In cases where the parties knowingly enter into an extramarital arrangement, they have certainly set themselves up to participate in hurt and pain. Even if it is not their own hurt and pain, someone will feel hurt and pain.

The person cheating on his or her significant other is dishonest with the significant other. The person who agrees to cheat is agreeing to only have access when the significant other is unavailable. This is hurtful. They usually don't trust the other person to be faithful, either.

In the extremely rare occasion when cheaters leave their significant other and enter a committed relationship with the person they were cheating with, there is a trust issue in the foundation of the relationship. The new significant-others know all of the things the cheaters did and said to free themselves up to be with them behind the back of their significant others. They are always on the look-out for those behaviors.

Please note that it is extremely rare that a person will leave the one they are with and enter into a committed relationship with the person he or she is cheating with. If they leave at all, they typically do not enter a relationship with the person they have been cheating with. They will enter a relationship with someone totally different.

Whether conscious or unconsciously, they have lost respect for the person they have been cheating with. They recognize that this person knowingly accepted less and facilitated their dishonesty and lack of integrity. I don't know anyone who wants to be in a long-term relationship with someone who *knowingly accepts less from them and facilitates their dishonesty*!

In our soul, we want someone who inspires us to be better. We want someone who brings out the best in us, not the worst. Most people also want a person who has self-respect. It is clear that there is no self-respect when you knowingly accept the position of side-chick or boy-toy. Remember this, whatever position you accept, is likely the position you will always hold for that person. I don't care what they *say*, they perceive you and have placed you in that position and they likely will always have you in that position.

If it is a position that you don't see yourself in long-term, then you should not accept it from the beginning unless you don't expect to be in the situation long-term. People often enter a situation thinking they will just hit-it-and-quit-it. The problem is that they stay too long. This is where the danger of hurt and pain for everyone enters the picture. This is not just true for cheating situations. It is true for the classic booty-call arrangement as well.

We will discuss this a little later. However, entering a sexual relationship with a casual approach for a short time is a dangerous proposition. More often than not, what starts off with the intention of being short-term becomes so convenient and even exciting because it is your *little secret* that the hunter gets captured by the game and now feelings become involved.

Someone wants more. Or, at a minimum, it is now six months later and that hit-it-and-quit-it situation is now a full-blown affair. This describes a situation where you knew you were on the Highway that could lead to hurt, but you thought you knew where all of the hurtful landmarks were and knew how to stay away from them. The problem is that the Highway takes twists and turns that you never knew existed. There are always new stops being built all the time. What you thought you knew and could handle has now been moved to a different location and in its place is this new shiny building that you think is safe to enter. Proceed with extreme caution.

Another building block in the foundation of a relationship that is sure to crack in the future is the relationship built on need vs. want. Some people need to be needed. They seek out people to help, change and save. They also sabotage that person's progress so that they remain the driving force and controlling factor in the relationship. Some people are down on their luck and need somewhere to stay and someone to help them survive. These are not good reasons to enter a relationship with someone, unless this is your job. If this is the foundation upon which an intimate, personal relationship is built, it is clearly being built on the Hurt People Highway.

As I said previously, the best chance for a healthy relationship that is likely to last, is for the two people who enter the relationship to be healthy. A person in need of basic survival means is not a healthy person with whom to be in a relationship. If I can't survive on my own, I have no business trying to add another person onto my plate. Period.

If the strongest motivation for being with someone is that you need a place to stay, this is not a good reason to be with them. In short, it is usury. The minute the crisis is over and you are back on your feet, whatever flaws or annoying habits the person has are likely to become more annoying. This will likely cause friction in the relationship. If you now have the means to get out you probably will. Yes, you used the person to get on your feet and left them on the Hurt People Highway.

Let me be clear. As a woman, I do not want a man that cannot provide basic survival needs. As women, we all want to feel safe in the hands of the man that we are with. It is one of the reasons that women are attracted to the bad-boy. It is not simply because he is bad, it is because he represents someone that will make sure we have food on the table, even if it means doing something less than legal, he will defend us against any physical attack and usually, he has a guard around his heart which we know means he is not likely to give access to that most special part to just anyone. That means that if we have access to his heart, it is safe to put ours there with his. He is on guard. Now this comes with a lot of other things that we don't want or factor in if we are new to the game, but underneath it all, this is usually why women are attracted to the bad-boy type.

There is a difference in wanting a partner who contributes his or her resources to ensure that our basic needs are met and the person that needs your resources to survive. Throughout history, families have arranged marriages because they needed the families to be joined financially. These marriages were often very unfulfilling and unhappy. Our instinct and sensibilities tell us that the person we are married to should be the person we want to share our most intimate feelings and secrets with. This should not be a person who was thrust upon us because the family needed money and for whom we have no interest or compatibility.

It is not a good feeling for anyone to realize that *but for the fact that you need what I have, you would not be with me.* It implies that you don't really want to be with ME. You want to be with WHAT I HAVE. Instinctively, we know that if fulfilling a need is the primary motivation for being in the relationship, once

Identifying the Elements

that need no longer exists, the need for me no longer exists. It also is a breeding ground for abuse, emotional and otherwise.

Men like to feel that the woman they are with *needs* them in their lives. If they perceive that a woman is self-sufficient, they are less interested. It was not that big of a challenge prior to women working regularly to support themselves financially. It creates a lot of open conflict, but a lot less is actually discussed because men simply walk away or never solidify a relationship with the woman that they perceive does not need them.

The fallacy in this mind-set is that it fails to recognize that women ALWAYS -- yes ALWAYS -- need men. Even in same-sex relationships, one partner is always more dominant and always assumes the masculine role. While a woman may not need a man for his financial support, we ALWAYS need a man for his emotional support. We need men for sex. We need men for their physical strength. More important than any of the reasons we need men in our lives, we WANT men in our lives. We want them to cherish and adore us. We want them to respect us. Regardless of our occupation or financial competence, we want men in our lives. We may not be willing to tolerate loveless, disrespectful, unfulfilling, transactional existences to have them in our lives, but I have never met a successful woman who does not want a man in her life.

Understand that a self-sufficient woman was probably left no choice. No knight in shining armor came to provide her basic necessities or she decided to do something that she was interested in for

Identifying the Elements

survival. She did not believe that she should live her life without owning a home or driving the car she wanted to drive because no man stepped up to the plate to provide those things for her. She simply got out there and got them for herself. I can almost certainly assure you that if a man had provided the things she wanted or needed, she would gladly have accepted them. There are, of course, exceptions to every rule. But they are just that, exceptions. I don't care how powerful you perceive a woman to be, she would much prefer to have a man to do the heavy lifting, physically and otherwise. She would much prefer to have a man to depend on.

An unfortunate side effect of women having to, or choosing to, do for themselves is that innately, these are masculine traits. Once a woman has been required to do all of the providing and protecting of herself and her children, her sensibilities become more masculine, if nothing else, in the eyes of men. Men automatically assume that she does not know how to follow a man or lean on a man and perceive her as being bossy or controlling.

Let me state for all of the self-sufficient women that I know, to all of the men that may ever read this or hear about this -- control of you is NOT our highest aim. If we were able to have control over you, that and about $4 might get us a cup of coffee at Starbucks.

I have always been amazed at men who thought I wanted to control them or be in control of the relationship. I was forced to raise my son as a single mother. I was forced to buy a home for myself. I was forced to earn my own money. These things were not my choices. My ex-husband has confirmed on more than one occasion that he just wasn't ready to be a responsible husband, we were very young, and that I had been a good wife to him and a great mother to our son.

Once I had a son, I was responsible. That meant he needed food, clothing and shelter. Those things were not optional. If my husband was not going to provide them, I had to. I always wanted to own a home. I earned enough money to buy one. I provided that dream for myself. I assumed a leadership role in the non-profit that I worked at when my Mommy passed away. I was the only person who knew enough about almost everything going on there to keep the organization going. That made me the boss.

I didn't want to let all of the work she had done or the projects that had yet to be completed just die because she made her transition. I wanted her legacy to survive. It took ten years to complete all of the projects that she had in the pipeline when she passed. With these factors as motivation, I became the head of the organization. I became the boss. In truth, I am most comfortable in the number-two position. It is, as I like to call it, my sweet spot. I discovered this about myself while working for my Mommy. I liked assisting her with bringing her vision to life and helping to make her ideas better. It didn't require the ultimate responsibility. I have adjusted to the ultimate responsibility position, but it would not be my choice.

For the man who has met a woman that appears to be too independent and that independence is the sole deterrent to being with her, check her history. More than likely, you will find that she has been carrying the load by herself for a very long time. She does not know what it is like to have someone to depend on. She does not know how and when to utilize help. She's not used to having any help for anything. If she is what you would choose except for this, take the time to explain to her that you recognize that she is used to having to do for herself and what role you intend to fill. This will be much more effective than accusing her of always wanting to be in control. Whenever someone is accused of anything, they become defensive and real communication becomes difficult. Know this, however. She will not likely be the one to relinquish responsibility to a person that has not demonstrated that he or she can be trusted. It is important to remember that she has had responsibility and authority imposed on her by people who did not live up to theirs.

Her willingness to now let everything she has been able to piece together, hold together, acquire or maintain into the hands of someone who has not demonstrated that they can be relied upon for simple things -- like calling when you say you will or showing up on time regularly -- won't be high.

It doesn't matter what you think of what she has. Whether she has only been able to maintain a public housing apartment on food stamps or an empire, if she wants to be with you, she will submit to your direction and advice once she is convinced that you will do no harm to what she has built. More importantly, she wants to be sure you won't hurt her heart.

Think of anything you do at the beginning of the relationship, that you know is likely to develop into a problem in the future, as you building the foundation on the Hurt People Highway, a road full of sinking-sand mines all along the way. Who does that?! Why would anyone want to do that?

Why would I build my foundation on a plot of land that is known to shift and sink. In most localities, the entity that approves new buildings makes the proposed builder get what is called a soil-analysis as part of the structural plan review, to ensure that the soil is capable of handling the weight of the structure being proposed. This is a separate, distinct review. In some cases, the soil is not sufficient on its own so they require the builder to strengthen the soil by importing and compacting other soil with it or additives before they can even think about building a foundation on it.

Then, the size of the foundation may have to be changed to ensure that the building does not collapse over time. Maybe if we looked at the beginning of our relationship as a soil-analysis and structural review we would not have so many collapses. Just a thought.

• *Fear*

Fear as a main ingredient in a relationship is unhealthy. Whenever people are motivated by fear, they don't make the best decisions. Anxiety about whatever it is we fear will, or will not happen, clouds our judgment. It is difficult to think when we are afraid. This is true in general. Add to that affairs-of-the-heart and sound decision-making is even harder to achieve.

There are lots of reasons that people have fear in relationships. My fear was that the person would leave, which stemmed from my belief that my father's continued love and presence was not guaranteed. There is fear that comes from being subjected to violence. There is fear that comes from being abandoned. There is fear that is the result of knowing that the relationship is built on a lie that was told and may be exposed. There is fear that comes from being afraid that a good relationship is finally here and it may not last.

It does not matter what *brand* of fear is constant in the relationship. It is unhealthy. It causes us to make poor decisions about simple and complex things. A woman who is afraid her husband will beat her may hesitate to tell him things that she believes will upset him. Important things often require immediate attention. Delay can be costly. However, because she is afraid of his anger and wrath, she may make a poor decision. A man who is afraid a woman will abandon him like his drug-addicted mother did, may panic when he cannot reach his mate for an hour. The possibilities for poor outcomes are endless when behavior is motivated by fear.

I exposed myself to pain because I did not set the appropriate boundaries for fear that the relationship would end. The worst part about that is -- IT ENDED ANYWAY. More often than not, the law-of-attraction dictates that the thing we focus on most is what will manifest. We get the very thing we don't want because we spend so much time being afraid of it that we concentrate on it. We anticipate the behavior we don't want to see happening. We obsess over it. This almost guarantees we will see it in the flesh. Every relationship is not the one that hurt us, unless we make it so by focusing on it all the time. We do this by attracting the similar behavior and then receiving the same outcome. It becomes a self-fulfilling-prophesy.

As I previously shared, the best gift I received from my relationship with the man who was incarcerated was that I loved *without fear*. I had learned enough throughout my lifetime about how to behave so that I lessened the chance that I would be subjected to a lot of hurt and pain.

Specifically, I only did things I wanted to do. I only gave what I wanted to give and what I could afford to give emotionally or physically. In short, I was intentional about my giving, loving, sharing and actions in the relationship. I took full responsibility for what I did or did not do in the relationship.

Secondly, my self-confidence was strong enough that I never felt that I had to be anything other than me in the relationship for it to be enough. The man made that extremely easy as well. Despite the harsh realities of the life he had lived to that point, he was very loving and had a huge heart. I found it amazing that he cared so much about things, even the other inmates. He was still able to see the beauty in others and in nature.

But more than anything he did, I just wasn't afraid to love him, share or express that love to him or anyone else. Another huge factor was that I just wasn't concerned about what anyone thought about me, him or the love we shared and what it looked like to them.

Other people's opinions didn't matter. I did not involve other people in deciding how I felt about it. I knew that people would think I was crazy because I have a successful career and was fifteen years older than him and he was incarcerated. What could there possibly be of any value in him for me? Once he was released from prison, this was part of why he didn't continue with the relationship. He didn't feel like he had anything to offer me. What he didn't realize was that all that I really needed and wanted from him was his heart and he had already given me that. If he had simply been consistent in his presence, everything else would have been fine. Recognizing that his low self-esteem, self-doubt and identity crisis were why he couldn't stay helped to ease the pain of the failed relationship. I will always treasure the time that I was able to love without fear.

- *Emotional and physical abuse*

It almost seems unnecessary to have to explain that any form of abuse in a relationship is unhealthy. It does not matter which party inflicts the abuse. I have seen women verbally and emotionally abuse their partners. Heck, I have seen women physically abuse their partners. I have to make it clear that abuse by anyone in a relationship is abuse and it is unhealthy. It certainly goes hand-in-hand with fear. Fear and intimidation are key elements in abuse. Intimidation is used to control. The fear of abusive behavior is used to control. Universal spirit law does not allow humans to control other humans.

In fact, we are lucky when we gain some measure of control over ourselves. But the ability to control others is not given to us. We may inspire others to action, but we can't control their behavior. Just watch parents with their children, it proves this. Even aggressive parents can't control what their children do once they are not in their presence. Abusers instinctively know this, so one of the first things they do in setting up their abusive reign over their abused is to isolate them from as much of the outside world as they can.

They find ways to limit contact with friends and family, they limit where the other person goes without them present, they limit how much time the other person spends at work as best they can. The intention is to isolate and program the person to believe that they are the answer to all of their questions in life. They are what is needed. They are the only people who truly cares. Without them, there is no life to be lived. It is all deception.

When we don't know our value and esteem ourselves so little, it is easy for someone to convince us that he or she is the answer to all of our needs and questions. Abusers start off building up the person they eventually abuse. They sense whatever need the other person has and begin to fulfill it, at the beginning. Once they have successfully lured their prey, they subtly begin to change. If they know that sex is the thing that makes their prey feel loved and happy, they begin to dole it out as reward for behavior they seek. They dole it out in exchange for control.

Identifying the Elements

Consider this. When the Creator created the creature who was most like Him, the one he created in his *image* (meaning he looks like Him) and his *likeness* (meaning having his traits and abilities), He did not retain for Himself the ability to control its every move by giving him **free will**.

It means that despite having breathed the very breath of life into man, He did not retain control over his every action. He gave us choice. It is the reason that people strongly resist being controlled. It is not in our nature to be controlled by others. When we allow another person to control our actions, it is destined to fail. It is an ability that the Creator did not choose for us. Anything that is in opposition to how that thing was created must fall. It cannot stand.

Often, people that witnessed abuse in their family become victims of abuse and/or abusers. Some people who are abused learn how to retaliate in small ways, ways that are abusive nonetheless. It becomes a vicious cycle. In order to break the cycle of abuse, people have to learn that it is not healthy. It becomes normalized in families. This has to be exposed as a lie in order for it to be changed. People don't stop what they don't find offensive.

- *Addiction*

One of the definitions of addiction is: *persistent compulsive use of a substance known by the user to be harmful*

There is ample proof that addiction to substances such as alcohol, drugs and food have a negative impact on the quality of life of the person addicted to them and their families. The devastation to the communities of color from the crack-addiction epidemic and now to the majority communities from the opioid-addiction epidemic is readily documented. You don't have to look to books, television or even the internet to see that these addictions are unhealthy and lead to devastating consequences for everyone they touch. You simply have to look in your own neighborhood and there is certainly a live, in-person example of the negative effects that substance addiction have on people, families and communities.

However, addiction to being in a relationship or *the relationship* is slightly different, but equally as devastating. Consider how I described my behavior in the most painful relationship I have ever experienced. I threw my pride, dignity and self-respect out the window to stay in the relationship. I continued to participate in the relationship even though I knew it was causing me pain. I put him before me. I needed and wanted him morning, noon and night. Those are persistent compulsive use of behavior (a substance) known by the user (ME) to be harmful.

I knew that every time I wanted him to be with me at an event and he said no, it hurt my feelings. I knew that when he refused to make a commitment to me that it hurt me. I knew that the fear of losing him was unnerving to me. I also knew that these things kept me on pins and needles. They kept me uneasy. I was not at peace. Those things were harmful. Yet, for years, I participated in persistent compulsive use. I was a bona fide addict.

The problem with being addicted to *a relationship* is that it destroys all boundaries and can become chaotic. Like substance abuse, the more the user partakes, the more unmanageable their lives become. The longer I stayed in the relationship, the less manageable it became. The more frequent the hurt came. The easier it became for him to disregard my feelings. The more harmful to me it became. Like substance addiction, I could not recover until I wanted help. There were times throughout the relationship that I broke it off, but relapsed and went back for more. He would pursue me with things he knew I wanted and I would fall right back into the relationship again. I had to, like any other addict, simply get tired of serving the addiction.

The truth is that if I continued, it could have led to death. Such a high percentage of women incarcerated are incarcerated as the result of the relationship they were in. The crime involves an intimate partner. Remember, I looked at insanity and thought it might not be that bad because I could no longer handle the hurt and pain.

The behaviors are the exact same behaviors of someone addicted to a substance. It is more sinister in some ways, though. In general, we do not connect behavior and willing participation in a relationship with addiction. Therefore, we don't see the need to avoid the substance. More often than not, we think it will get better. In other words, we think we can manage it. We don't see that we are doing harm to ourselves, or those around us. When our loved ones see us continue to set ourselves up for the same hurt as the last time, it is difficult for them to watch. They

Identifying the Elements

are helpless in getting us to see that our behavior is destructive. Just like a substance-addict. We believe that people are "just hating" on our relationship. They don't want to see us happy. Then we dig our heels in in defiance of what we think is someone being jealous instead of listening to what they are saying. We don't see the relationship as an addiction or a substance that from persistent compulsive use is causing us harm.

- *Situationship vs. relationship*

I have coined a phrase "situationship" for all of the various ways that people are relating and dealing with each other that have elements of a relationship but in reality, they have nothing. We all know people who talk and behave as if they are in a relationship with someone but they are the only one in the relationship. The other person is in a situation with them. The dealings are one-sided. The two only get together when one person wants to or can fit the other in. There is no real commitment or definition, yet one party behaves as if he or she has a spouse. They treat the other person like royalty, yet they are the last on the list of the person they treat so well.

If you are in a situation with a person who wants to spend time with you but only in private, never around other people, they do not include you in the rest of their life, they say they don't believe in titles, you are last on their priority list, you are often disappointed that they only agree to do things with you that they want to do and never when you want to and ultimately, you can not depend on their presence or support but they will engage in sexual relations with you, you are in a situationship, not a relationship.

I recall a man who asked to take me to dinner. He wanted to get to know me and spend time with me. He took me to Roscoe's Chicken and Waffles in Los Angeles, at my request. After he took me to dinner, he sent me a few text messages and suddenly began to refer to me as his girl. I was stunned. I kept thinking, "He thinks he got all of this fabulousness for a chicken dinner and a few text messages?"

I could not believe that he was claiming me, without even asking if I wanted to be his girl for so little an investment. So I mentioned it to my co-worker in our lunchroom one day. I just couldn't get over it. She listened and explained that there were lots of girls who would fight me over him once he did those things for them and claimed them.

I refused to believe that she was telling me the truth. I told her she was just being funny. She was much younger than me, like my daughter, and we would tease each other, so I thought she was just teasing me. We leave the lunchroom and we bring another co-worker into the conversation. Without my young co-worker saying a word, the other co-worker, who is older than me, commented that there were women who would fight me about him if he did those things for them. I could not believe that she believed the same thing. They believed it because they had seen women who were in situationships claim relationships too many times before and were willing to do bodily-harm to anyone who would try to mess with "their man."

I think I'm still shocked at the reality that there are people who will allow someone to claim them and they have not invested any time or real effort into proving that they are worthy or what the other person is entitled to. In my mind, I wanted to know what that obligated me to do. What am I now responsible for after a chicken dinner and a couple text messages? Surely, it can't be that much. Well, the worst part is that some women who have accepted that chicken dinner and two or three text messages have committed themselves to allowing a man access to their time, home, body, finances and heart for the low-low price of a few hours of attention. These are situationships. Once the commitment is obtained for so little investment, minimal time and effort at best, the woman then claims to be in a relationship and the man can proceed to line up other women in the same way.

Men are prey as well. They meet a woman who they really want to be in a relationship with and pursue her. She wants the benefit of their time and entertainment, but does not want to be with *them*. Since they make themselves and their resources available, she makes use of them. She often pretends to be virtuous, which is why she can't fully give herself to him sexually and this makes him believe he has found the woman of his dreams.

While she is pretending virtuous-ness with him, she is playing the harlot with other men. The things that she denies this man, she is doing or will do with another man. While she makes excuses for not escorting him to family functions, she is breaking out her Sunday-best to attend a family event with another man. Even if the other man is not in her life at that moment, as soon as she meets a man who she believes is what she really wants, she is no longer available to this man.

When the man who believes he has found his queen tells the story of their dealings and relations, he is genuinely excited and clearly smitten with her. Because he is giving her all that he has and she appears to be receiving it, he believes they are in a real relationship. The problem is that it is only in appearance and he has yet to see that the behavior is not consistent with the appearance and it is one-sided. In reality, they are in a situationship, not a relationship.

• *Who do we have relations or dealings with?*

There are three broad categories of relations and dealings between men and women that involve or have involved sexual relations. It is necessary to isolate the sexual nature of these relations and dealings because it is the one behavior that generally distinguishes the nature of these relationships from other male-female relationships such as father-daughter, brother-sister, friend-friend, colleague-colleague dealings.

I have male friends in my life who we are blessed to share conversations about our deepest desires for our lives and families, our disappointments and accomplishments and our greatest joys. These are intimate relationships, but they are not sexual and never have been. So the behavior that makes men and women view their dealings and relations with particular men and women differently, is sex. It is the most intimate behavior two people can share. Yet today, people engage in sex very casually.

Men have an ability to engage in sex on a transactional basis more readily than women. It can be just for the act itself. They have the ability -- for a longer time than women, to continue to see the sex act as merely that.

Make no mistake, however, that after a period of time, whether you are male or female, continued engagement in sexual relations will produce an emotional attachment. I did not say love, but an emotional attachment. Women don't have the ability to remain emotionally unattached for as long as men. While women may begin a purely sexual relationship believing they can handle it being purely sexual, if the encounters are frequent, she will develop an emotional attachment.

This is the source of a lot of hurt and pain for women. Once we have given ourselves in this manner, it stirs up emotions that become very strong. The reason is pretty simple yet people don't seem to know it or they ignore the power of it. We ignore the power, despite having seen the sometimes-violent reactions of people upon finding out that the person they are having sex with is having sex with someone else. People have killed people for this.

The reason we cannot continue to engage in sexual behavior without becoming emotionally attached is because it is the most sacred part of us that we have to give to another person. I don't care how new-aged or sexually-liberated a woman is, if she continues to give herself to a man sexually, she will develop an emotional attachment. Somehow she will begin to believe that she should be receiving special consideration in his life.

I know of several women who have engaged in a casual sexual relationship with a particular man. They know and agree that there is no commitment to the relationship. They know that they will only see this man when they are planning to have sex. Even if they dress it up and go to dinner and a movie ahead of time, it is only the prelude to get to the sex. It is a ritual. They agree to this and participate. They know that the man has sex with other women.

However, when confronted with the *reality* of this fact, like finding the other woman's personal items at his home or finding out that he is with her at an event, their feelings are hurt, they feel disrespected and become emotional.

I always had a hard time understanding how you could knowingly agree to have sex with a man who was having sex with other women and then be upset about the fact that he is having sex with other women.

Never made sense until I realized that it is the one thing we have that we don't give to everyone we meet. We know that it should be reserved for special people. Like our fanciest dress, we don't wear it every day or to just any gathering, it is reserved for "special" occasions.

Additionally, we were not created to share this most intimate part of ourselves with everyone. After Adam and Eve ate the fruit of the tree of the knowledge of good and evil in the Bible, they immediately sewed fig leaves together and covered their genitals. It was an indication of a new consciousness that it is inappropriate to share this area of the body with everyone. It was an indication that it is the most sacred part of us that we can share with another person and it signifies becoming one with another human.

I don't know what it will take for people to recognize that no matter how strong you are or how many notches you have on your proverbial belt, you cannot engage in regular sexual contact with another person and not develop an emotional attachment.

It is not always the woman who wants more from the arrangement after time. Sometimes a man will start off having multiple women in this way when he chooses. It is all fun and games. He is not misleading anyone, he gets to choose which woman he spends time with and under what circumstances. He is living the life, all the way up until the day that he's not. He finds himself dialing the same number more than the others. Maybe the other women have already gotten off the train. Maybe the ultimate sin was committed; she had sex with another man. Suddenly he's not having fun anymore. He becomes angry. He's angry because he thought he had it all figured out and it was his territory.

Men are hunters and gatherers by nature. Once they have gathered a woman, as it were, they don't take kindly to another man trying to gather her. That is why once a man has claimed a woman for himself, even after the relationship ends, he continues to claim her for himself.

Identifying the Elements

How many men have told a woman that she was "always gonna be his." What? How does that work when you are married to another woman? How did I get a life-sentence and you have another life? It does not make rational sense, but these affairs are not conducted in the rational realm because they involve something that we know is more sacred and should not be shared casually. We know it instinctively, even if we have never thought of it intellectually. Even if we have never been taught to keep this part of us sacred, we know it. Even when a man has to urinate on the side of the road, he turns his back away from the road so that no one will see his penis. If he did not instinctively believe that it was not supposed to be viewed by the world, he would not position himself so that no one could see it while doing something that is not only natural, but required by the body. Constant sharing of the most sacred part of us generates emotional attachment. Period.

In general, as I said, there are three broad categories of intimate relationships where men and women engage in sexual relations: spouse/significant other; co-parent/baby mama or daddy; and casual sexual partner/booty call. Each one requires a different standard of care and attention. Each has different rules, if you will. There are rules and levels to this sexual relationship thing. While each of these three categories involves or has at some point in time involved sexual dealings, they are not all created equal and do not require the same level of care and attention.

In fact, it is this reality that usually causes great hurt and pain for the people engaged in these dealings because they often want the relationship to be something that it is not. People also provide access and service consistent with much more than they are receiving in benefit. When they realize that it is not what they envisioned it to be, after they have been involved for months and often years, they are hurt. We can stop this vicious cycle. Let's examine the three types.

- *Spouse, significant other*

A spouse is defined as *a married person*. This is a relationship where two people have declared before an officiate that they are going to be legally joined. This is the highest level of responsibility and should come with the greatest benefit.

Let's face it. It is hard to share space with the same person day in and day out, year in and year out. It is hard work to remain excited about seeing the same person at the same level that you were excited in the beginning. Excitement settles and relationships evolve over time. We should never expect to feel the same giddiness after ten years that we do six months into the relationship.

A spouse is a person who you make all of the personal sacrifices that a relationship requires for. He or she is the person who you get out of bed in the middle of the night to go to the store for when you know you have to get up early in the morning, but they have a need.

This is the person who you sacrifice your personal needs and wants for because he or she is just that important and, very importantly, would do it for you. This is the *balance* part in the definition of healthy. People get married every day for all sorts of reasons, but remember I am talking about *healthy* relationships. There is no need to spend any time exploring how to get into and survive dysfunctional relationships. It is clear to me that the world has that down to a science. No need to read a book about that. Just look at reality-television shows. Plenty of dysfunction there.

These people also have legal standing with respect to each other. It may not seem like a big deal, but it is. It is a big deal in the positive and negative sense. That is why it should not be entered into lightly. For example, on the positive side, a spouse has the legal right to make medical decisions in the case of incapacitation, collect Social Security income and inherit things of value upon the death of their spouse.

On the other hand, they also are responsible for the debts left behind, often are jailed as co-conspirators whether they were involved or not in illegal financial conspiracies and in some of the most extreme cases of the down-side of being legally married, have been injured or killed by someone because their marriage is an inconvenient legal barrier to someone else's plans.

A significant other is a term that has become popular in the past decade or so to describe the relations between two people who appear to be committed to each other but have not taken the legal steps to be called spouses. The word *significant* is defined as *having meaning; having or likely to have influence or effect, important*. It should be clear from

Identifying the Elements

the very definition how this person should be treated. It is interesting to note that the term was coined to impress upon observers that these people who are not legally tied to each other have a commitment and hold a place of meaning and importance in each other's lives.

This is automatically implied with the legal, binding nature of becoming a spouse. One of the reasons that people remain a significant other is because they don't want the legal responsibility of marriage. Often, people want to be important to others and committed to them, but not responsible for their debts, nor put them in a position to take their assets should the relationship fail.

I have seen couples purchase property and build assets together but remain unmarried for years. For some couples it works. I have never understood the psychological side of doing everything that a married couple does, including building financial ties, but wanting to remain legally untied. I know that there is some psychological reason for it. Usually, in trying to get an explanation from people as to why they do this, it boils down to something that the couples would argue is not true, but no matter how you dress it up, it amounts to the fact that underneath it all, they don't trust the other person with legal responsibility.

They don't want to be responsible for the other person's financial holdings or they don't want the other person to have legal access to their financial holdings. These couples often even have children together, spend decades together, but when it comes to legally committing to each other, they stop short.

Identifying the Elements

Psychologically, they can always leave, even though that is not factually true. Once you have children together, move in together, buy cars and real estate together, there is no easy way out. In some states, there are community-property laws that give men and women who have lived together and invested more than seven years the same legal rights as spouses upon separation. So the misguided idea that there is always an easy exit because there is no legal marriage is not necessarily true. As mentioned previously, it can backfire because unless these couples put their desires on paper, upon death or incapacitation, the person who has invested years in the relationship suddenly has no say over anything legally.

If they own property together, the 50 percent interest of the deceased or incapacitated person is inherited by family members. They may not be able to take the real estate, but they certainly may have the right to require their 50 percent value be paid out. I am too conservative about my money to put myself in that kind of legal jeopardy. If I am going to invest financially with someone that I am sharing myself with emotionally, there must be some written, legal documentation of our intentions. If I am in business with someone, there is a written agreement to describe our intentions. I am not willing to take the chance that there is any misunderstanding between us later or that the person dies and his heirs have no idea about our intentions.

So I certainly cannot see myself living as a spouse without legal benefits. The truth is, these couples assume all of the responsibility and benefits without the legal protections. It should be absolutely clear that if you are not a legally married person, you are not a spouse. If you are not actually engaged, you are not a fiancé. Yes, I said it. If you don't have a ring on it, you are neither a spouse nor a fiancée.

You should not allow yourself to be called one, either. The problem with using these titles in situations where they are not actually true is that usually both parties are performing the duties associated with the titles and assume all of the responsibilities associated with the titles, but have none of the legal protections or benefits associated with them.

I acknowledge that the commitment of these roles must be in place before the actual ceremonies of either a fiancée or a spouse. However, it is unwise to accept the title of something that you are not. We only allow this because it implies that we have been chosen and are special. Let me prove it. If we attended a gathering with a person we are dating and they began to introduce us to their co-workers by saying: This is YOUR NAME, he or she is my paid escort, he or she is my side-piece.

We would be offended by that, unless it was true. Even if it were true, in most cases, we would not want to be introduced with those titles because they don't make us sound good. In fact, they make us sound cheap and unimportant. I offer that we should not accept titles that don't accurately reflect the nature of our relationship. If the commitment is real it is only necessary for the two people involved to have that understanding. If the two people have mutually agreed that they don't want the legal titles, that is their prerogative. However, it is disingenuous to each other, forget the rest of the world, to accept the responsibility for the sake of public appearances that you know you don't have.

If you only want to be a girlfriend or boyfriend while performing the duties and assuming the responsibilities of a spouse, that, again, is your prerogative, but why do you put up a front in public? Why not acknowledge your choice in public: This is YOUR NAME, she is my girlfriend of fifteen years? I say own it. I admire that about Oprah and Stedman. I have never heard either of them refer to the other as their fiancé.

They have acknowledged for themselves first, that they do not want to be legally married, and do not claim an engagement that has not happened and do not claim to be spouses. They are mature enough and secure enough in themselves to stand in the face of society and say they don't feel the need to subscribe to the norms of society or what would be expected of them. They consent to being in a relationship without the legal titles and they don't feel the need to mislead society about their choice. It is their relationship and their choice. I say kudos.

It has always been a pet peeve of mine when couples introduce themselves as fiancé. Yes, you've been together for six years, but you haven't put a ring on it nor set a date. Stop it. Ok, I've had my rant. I'm sure I have stepped on someone's toes here, but if we are to have healthy relationships, honesty is paramount. Honesty must be a building block, part of the foundation. If we are assuming the roles and responsibilities of a spouse and *want* to be a spouse, then we have to be honest enough to admit this. We have to require it.

I strongly advise against assuming the responsibilities and duties of a spouse when you are not, especially if you ever want to be a spouse. Everyone knows that no one is going to buy the cow when they can get the milk for free. If you ever want to be married, it is dangerous to move-in with your intended spouse without a clear understanding and time-frame that has been discussed. I would offer that if you strongly believe that you need to live together before marriage that you be legally engaged with a date set before you do so. This is not about what it looks like to society. It is about the psychological impact of giving someone the benefits of having you as a spouse without the responsibility.

I lived with my husband before marriage, and have lived with someone that I did not marry. It is based on these experiences that I offer this advice. Psychologically, I know that I carried the notion of always being able to walk away from the relationship into my marriage. I didn't feel like I had to "put up with anything" because we were married.

Well, marriage requires you to put up with things. It requires hard work and dedication. The commitment is for the long haul, through the good and bad. Psychologically, I just didn't take that into my marriage and when I felt he was not living up to his part of the deal, I ended it. The truth is that I had doubts about the marriage from the beginning because we were so young and he was financially irresponsible. I married anyway because I did love him and we had a child who I wanted to have the benefit of having a two-parent household.

Being so financially conservative, I have to admit that I did have doubts, but was willing to try for the "sake of my son." Well, I would strongly advise against doing that also. I was young and in love and wanted the fairytale. Deep down inside, however, I wasn't convinced that he would be able to live up to my fantasy. He loved me very much and proved it. We were engaged very quickly. Yes, the kind with the ring and date. Then I became pregnant and vanity would not allow me to walk down the isle pregnant so we postponed the wedding until after our son was born.

This brings me to another point worth making. Often people marry, for transactional reasons, a person who is in no other way important or influential to them. This is a tragedy for both parties and certainly any children they have. It robs both parties of the opportunity to have a real marriage. I have heard people say that marriage is a business arrangement. Only marriages in which the parties don't want to put in the work to be married or when it is, from the beginning, a business arrangement.

Throughout history people have married for money and status. It was a business arrangement from the beginning. However, when couples don't have any money to speak of and allow their marriages to be reduced to a series of business transactions like cooking and cleaning, paying bills, sex only when necessary and there is no real interest in each other's lives, the people are usually miserable.

Identifying the Elements

There is something missing and it becomes hurtful. They become trapped in a situation that they don't feel special in but they feel obligated. It is unhealthy for the children because they do not grow up seeing what a healthy couple looks like. In fact, they get the wrong idea of what a marriage and parenting looks like. It is harder to un-teach unhealthy ideas and habits than it is when there is no image of what a relationship should look like. It is always easier to write on a clean slate than to erase what is there and start over.

These kinds of marriages produce generational unhappiness because they normalize and model for the children unhealthy interaction. Think again about children who grow up in a home with domestic violence. They often become victims or victimizers. It doesn't have to be that extreme to pass along unhealthy relationship habits to the next generation. The way we communicate displeasure or disappointment. Parents are programming the next generation how to respond to disappointment, anger, frustration and the like.

This is how they will cope when these things arise in their own lives. If the response is to shut down and fail to communicate it until I am no longer angry, then that is what the children will model. I will say it a million times. I believe that staying in an unhealthy situation for the sake of the children is a really poor choice. It causes long-lasting damage because it teaches that it is acceptable to suffer and be unimportant in your own home.

- *Baby mamas or daddies*

Today, people raise children with people who they are not married to. It is such a common occurrence that the phrases "baby's mama" and "baby's daddy" have been coined. This becomes a reality when couples divorce. The single parent rightfully should be called my ex-wife or ex-husband in those cases. In the situations where they have never been married, the phrases apply. The situations can become extremely unhealthy for a number of reasons. We can start with the way the situation is created. Two people who are not married and don't have a legal commitment to each other have sex. They have unprotected sex, to be specific. The result is a pregnancy. The choice is to have the child. This may not be so bad when the two people have been in a "significant other" relationship because they know each other and intend to be with each other.

Knowing each other is crucial when deciding to bring another person into the relationship and the world. Having a child is a life sentence. There will never be another time in life when the two people producing the child will not be connected in some way. They will forever be the parents of the child. So just as people join two families when they marry, they are joining two families when they have a child. I strongly suggest, no urge, people to be careful who you have children with. There is no divorcing children. Children need both parents. If children are to grow up healthy, no matter how you feel about the other parent, the children NEED them to feel whole, safe, healthy and loved. It does not matter how you feel about that. It is a fact.

When I realized that my ex-husband and I were not going to stay married, I became a single parent. My son had the best possible scenario being raised by a single parent because he had regular interaction with my brothers and other men, all of whom showed him love, kindness, validation and examples of manhood.

However, the truth is, none of it mattered because HIS father was not consistent in his life. He moved out of state and was not consistent in his communication with his son. This caused a great deal of hurt and anger in my son. This affected him in his life and in particular, his view of the world. It made him less trusting of people. I can understand why. If the person who created you does not live up to their responsibility toward you, how can you realistically expect anyone else in the world to do so?

Despite the interest shown him by several positive male role models, they were not his father. It caused him harm. My son did not go hungry or lack anything other than having his father in his life. Many people would look at his childhood and say that he lived a very good life. I agree, but it doesn't matter because his father was not consistent in his life and that is the other half of who he is and it left a hole in his foundation.

Children blame themselves for why the other parent is not in their lives. They don't know the dealings between the parents. Even if they see the parents argue frequently, they don't understand all of the dynamics and they internalize the conflict and

Identifying the Elements

believe it has something to do with them. The reality is that it never really has anything to do with them. It is the drama of the parents that causes them not to be civilized enough to put the child's needs above their own.

So often in these relationships, the parents, who never knew each other and were never really in a healthy relationship to begin with, are angry at each other and the child becomes a pawn in the dangerous game being played between the two. Some situations, as I said, are the product of people who were in a relationship that never matured to a legal marriage but they knew each other and cared for each other. These scenarios can produce a healthy co-parenting relationship. The problem today is that more often than not, the parents were never in a relationship but engaged in behavior that should be reserved for people who are.

They do not use birth control, which is totally irresponsible on the part of both people. Then, once the pregnancy occurs, they expect the situation to turn into a healthy co-parenting arrangement. Usually, the man, who should have used a condom at minimum, accuses the woman of trying to trap him and is angry.

The woman, who should have used any number of available birth control methods, including a condom to prevent STD's, is angry at the man because he doesn't want to be a parent to her child and doesn't step up and become father-of-the-year. After the pregnancy happens, it is too late to become angry about your own irresponsible choices. Yes, abortion is an option, but these same, totally irresponsible people

Identifying the Elements

so often gain a moral compass and say they are against abortion.

They somehow now have principles that they believe so strongly in that they bring another person into the world to suffer at their hands for a lifetime because they will never be able to put aside their own egos and anger to create a healthy co-parenting situation. The child's life starts off in chaos and drama. It continues in drama and all either parent can do is focus on their issues. Once you bring the child into the world, your issues should take a backseat to the needs of the child. I was very angry at my ex-husband for not being a consistent parent to my son. We were engaged, I was not necessarily ready to have a child, but I engaged in irresponsible behavior and a child was produced. He was ecstatic. I wasn't unhappy about it. I became unhappy when he did not become responsible for my son above his own wants.

As an irresponsible young woman, I should have known better because he had already shown that he was not responsible in some ways. He was not a bad person, simply irresponsible. I should not have expected him to miraculously become a responsible parent when he wasn't a responsible person, even with his own affairs.

However, I always put aside my anger to try to facilitate visitations. I never, ever spoke ill of my son's father to him. I knew that he would be able to see his father's flaws on his own one day. It would not be productive to bad-mouth his father to him. Primarily, this is a bad idea because the things that are said to a child of a negative nature about the absent parent are translated to bad things about them. Children whose custodial parent is always bashing the absent parent believe that *they* are flawed just like the absent parent.

The things that the custodial parent spews in anger about the other parent become self-esteem issues for the children. I knew this and my mother never spoke ill of my father in front of me until she had no choice. Even then, she was delicate in how she presented it. I had a good role model for navigating a co-parenting situation. There were times when I simply could not stand the sight of my ex-husband. But because my son needed him, I would allow him to come to my home and spend time with his son. I would simply go to my bedroom and not come out until he was leaving. I don't suspect that he or my son knew that I was hiding from the anger I felt.

I was cordial and allowed them the run of my entire household so that they could have time together. Just as with my father, my son eventually came to know the realities of his father's flaws. I never needed to tell him anything. His father, like my own, continued to be who he was and, like me, my son began to understand his flaws and shortcomings.

His inconsistency became apparent to my son without me saying anything bad about him. I even spent time trying to explain to my son that his father did love him. He just didn't know how to express it and be consistent. His father's family was not close-knit like my family. My family got together for any reason or no reason at all. We spent lots of time with each other. His family was not close. His father lived in the home, but they did not have a close relationship. There was love, but not a lot of interaction.

So he parented the way he was parented. It makes a strong case for checking out the family dynamic of the person you are having sex with before deciding to have unprotected sex and bring a child into that life. I am going to step on some toes here. So, if you are sensitive, you may wind up feeling some type of way about what I am about to say. I want to discuss the role that women play in creating this, often unhealthy, environment for their children. So many women get involved with a married man or a man who has a significant other and think that having a child by them is going to somehow force them to leave their current situation and they will ride off into the happily-ever-after.

I am not sure what makes them think this, but these are the women that become the most angry and destructive toward the father of their children when the plan they devised doesn't work. They don't get the agreement of the man before they get pregnant. They simply make a life-choice for everyone and then have the nerve to get angry when the father does not want to parent their child.

They are really angry because the man did not leave the woman to be with them. I don't understand this concept. How can anyone be angry with a man for not doing what he never said he would? But these women are actually angry when the man does not do anything to support or nurture the child. Now, the man is as wrong as the woman to punish the child for the mistakes made by two adults. If a man has unprotected sex with a woman, he has to know that she could become pregnant. He is equally as responsible to nurture the child that he fathered. He must be an adult and live with the consequences of his behavior.

However, he NEVER has to be with the woman. He is even entitled to be angry at her choice to have a child that they never agreed to have. But he is responsible for the financial and emotional support of the child. Now, when he is not, the woman should not be surprised. She should not be surprised because if he is married, he was not living up to the vows he took with the woman he was with the day he met you. He was clearly demonstrating that he has no integrity. Now that you have had sex with him, you believe he found some in your vagina? I'm just asking a question. There is no question this is not a stand-up guy. He proved it to you simply by being with you. Even if he has never taken a legal vow, and is simply living with another woman and cheats with you, he has proven he is untrustworthy. He has proven that he will take the benefits without assuming full responsibility.

What makes you think he is going to be different with you? Why would you take this kind of chance with your child's life? You are setting them up to feel unloved and unwanted. It is a terrible way to begin a life. It creates life-long emotional challenges for humans when they feel unloved and unwanted by their parents.

Yet, people engage in unprotected sex and bring other little lives into this situation. If you don't believe in abortion, use birth control. If you don't believe in birth control, keep your clothes on instead of ruining another person's life. I don't feel sympathy for the mother or father in these situations. In short, grow up.

Once you have produced a child in this situation, you owe it to the child to do everything you can to co-parent in such a way that doesn't do further harm to the child. The father has to swallow hard, accept the consequences of his choice to have unprotected sex with a woman who was not their wife or significant other, and be a parent to the child both financially and emotionally.

The mother has to accept that the man will likely be very angry at her forever and may not treat this child with the same affection he would treat other children he has, but be very open to allowing and encouraging regular communication and visitation with the father.

She has to accept that she will not be a part of their interaction. Even when the children are small, she does not have to be there for the father to parent. Keeping the children away from their father, should he be responsible enough to recognize and fulfill their need, is not hurting the father, but hurting the child.

That damage is placed at the feet of the mother. She has to swallow her hurt and embarrassment that her plan did not work and she produced children with a man who doesn't want to be with her. She knew or should have known that he was not going to be with her because he was not AVAILABLE to be with her.

Even in circumstances when the man lies about his relationship status, we always find out the truth. When you find out the truth, take the appropriate steps to protect yourself. Don't continue a

185

Identifying the Elements

relationship with a person who is unqualified to be with you. He is disqualified from being with you by virtue of the fact that he is committed to someone else. I don't care how unhappily committed he is. He is committed and thus unqualified. No matter how you rearrange it, he is not qualified to be in a relationship with you. Most certainly, do not engage in unprotected sex and produce a child. It is a recipe for a lifetime of suffering for all parties involved.

Men, if you are going to cheat on the woman who you committed to, whether on the lowest level you can get away with -- living with her and not marrying her or have taken vows legally with her, use a condom. It is so irresponsible with everyone's life. Not only can you ruin the life of a child, you will surely break the heart of the woman you made a commitment to and it will never, ever be the same again. You may even give her a sexually transmitted disease that could cost her her life. Are all of these life-long consequences worth the thirty-second thrill? I say thirty-seconds because the really, really, really good part of sex only lasts about thirty-seconds. Time it if you have nothing else to do.

There is also the woman who knows the man has not been consistent in her life, nor has he promised her anything, but she allows herself to become pregnant and is angry that he is who he always was, irresponsible and inconsistent in the life of the child. If he has proven to be inconsistent in your life, then you should have no expectation that he will become those things because you allowed him to father your child. Often, such men had no role model in parenting They are not mature enough to be parents. So do not withhold the child from him because he is not consistent with financial support or even visitation. When he does find his responsible gene, don't put up roadblocks. Your child needs him. Your child needs the attention from this raggedy man who you chose to father them.

You also do not get to torture the child by reminding them that their father is irresponsible and inconsistent. Remember, YOU made the choice to engage in unprotected sex with an irresponsible, inconsistent man and further to bring a child into that situation. The child is the victim here, not you. Grow up. Live with your consequences, as well. The most unhealthy part of these relationships is the drama that follows the choice. No matter what choices were made that created a baby's mama/daddy situation, the adults' issues, desires, needs and wants become secondary to the needs of the child. Once you bring children into your situationship, you owe it to them not to mess up their lives with insecurity, low-self esteem, lack of confidence and worse because you made poor choices. Above everything the child should not be a piece in your board-game life. He or she should never be a pawn to be moved around to suit your fantasy. Stop the drama.

- *Casual sexual partners or booty calls*

These relationships are the most likely to be unhealthy because they involve two people sharing the most sacred thing they have to share with someone on a casual basis. As I have stated, two people are not likely going to be able to continually share this sacred experience and remain unemotional and detached. One party is always going to want more, eventually. One party is going to become unfulfilled with the sexual exchange that they *know* means nothing to the other person.

News flash here ladies: Men do not like to feel like a piece of meat. Even though they may engage in casual sex with women to fulfill a physical need and nothing more, they do not like to feel as if they are simply a piece of meat. The perfect depiction of this was in the movie *Boomerang*. Robin Givens' character has sex with Eddie Murphy's character and gets up and leaves him in his bed as if he was nothing more than a piece of meat. He was a womanizer. He was about that casual sex lifestyle. He knew how to do it, so he thought. For some reason, he felt cheap when she simply got up out of the bed and put on her clothes to leave.

I have seen this happen in life, as well. I also know that they do not like to be approached as if they are a piece of meat. A dear friend told me of a situation that offended him greatly. He was pumping his gas and a woman walked up to him and told him that he looked like he had a big penis and wanted to perform oral sex on him.

These were not the words she used. Her words were much more graphic. He was not flattered. He was offended. She gave him her telephone number and he promptly threw it away. He was not interested for a couple reasons. He was not interested because, as I've said, he did not like being treated like a piece of meat. He was not interested because he figured that if she was that aggressive with him in a gas station, she was likely to be that aggressive with other men and was a sexually dangerous choice.

He was clear to point out that she was an attractive woman. If she had presented herself like a lady she may have gotten to experience her fantasy with him, but instead she conducted herself like a predator and he was turned off. Despite the fact that this man is very attractive and is not in a committed relationship with anyone, he has a personal policy that requires him to wait to have sex with women. He may talk to various women regularly, but he does not engage in sex with all of them. He is actually quite selective. Most women who know him would have a hard time believing this. I am not sexually involved with him, so he is very open with me about this topic. He is often misperceived to be involved with lots of women sexually. It just isn't true.

The consequences of engaging in casual sex are hurt and pain for one or both people involved. It can lead to being in the previous category, which is sure to inflict pain on both parties and most importantly, the child. It can lead to sexually transmitted diseases. This is a minefield of hurt and painful consequences. The consequences can be as simple as being faced with the reality that you are nothing more than a sexual object to the other person. It is not a good feeling for anyone. It is the most intimate behavior we can engage in. We want to be appreciated for sharing that part of ourselves with someone. This is true even if it doesn't start off this way. If we continue to engage in this behavior, we expect it to take on meaning somewhere along the way.

Identifying the Elements

Speaking for myself, I had engaged in a sexual relationship on-and-off with a man for years. Sometimes it would be months of engagement and sometimes we would go years without contact. It just depended on whether we were in other relationships or not. However, at a point in my life, I wanted more from the relationship.

He was honest with me that what I created for him, a secret escape from his daily life to a place he could be comfortable, enjoy the company and have great sex before returning to his daily responsibilities, was good for him and he liked it that way. He also lived out-of-state and wasn't willing to attempt a long-distance relationship. I admired his honesty, but was hurt by its reality. I did not fault him for liking the fantasy world that I had created. I intentionally created that environment at the beginning. He was recently divorced and had a lot of other real challenges going on. My Achilles heel of always putting the issues and needs of the man ahead of what I need kicked in and I wanted to show understanding. I intentionally created a place for him to step off the world to. It was fine for a long time because we didn't see each other regularly enough for me to become emotionally attached at the beginning. He also always made it an experience. Through the years, I did become emotionally attached and wanted more.

Ok, here's a news flash for men: If you are going to be a booty call, you need to make it an experience every time. You need to bring your A-game. You can't be a booty call and a quickie at the same time. A quickie is for committed couples who will get back to the full experience when they can. It is to hold them over until they can get to it. You can NOT be a quickie and a booty call. By virtue of the fact that you are just a booty call, if the rules of this game are being honored, it means that you don't do this often and therefore there is an urgent need and you are the last resort.

Even if, like in the situation I am describing, this man was and remains one of my favorite sexual partners, you are there when there is a purely sexual need, you need to do your best to make it worth the effort and good enough to get to the next time. But the major point is that despite knowing that this relationship was merely a periodic sexual encounter with full disclosure at the beginning, it was hurtful to know that it would *never* be more than that when I wanted it to be.

The reality of sharing the most sacred, intimate part of ourselves with someone without the appropriate responsibility or rights is, likely, unhealthy. The foundation is unhealthy. We are mixing apples and oranges. We are taking a great chance that someone's feelings will get hurt. Someone will enter that Hurt People Highway because almost every encounter has something in it that leads to that road.

I didn't like the fact that there were times that I wanted to have my booty call and he simply wasn't available. I want what I want when I want it. It was hurtful that he wasn't available. That was a small hurt. Thankfully, because of my willingness to be honest with myself and not play the victim, I had to put on my big girl panties and accept the consequences of my actions. On more than one occasion over the years, it meant hurt feelings and disappointment. This is the nature of the booty call. So if you are into disappointment, this is the relationship for you. It is guaranteed to oblige your need.

Chapter 6

WHERE DO WE GO FROM HERE?

Now that we have identified the unhealthy elements of a relationship, where do we go from here? Ultimately, we go back to the beginning. We go back to the definition of healthy. We begin the journey through our unhealthy elements first and then the unhealthy elements of people we are in relationship with. We ensure that they are sound -- built on a good foundation, and balanced -- never catering to the needs of only one person, in both appearance and behavior.

• *The first relationship*

The most important relationship you have is with YOU. It begins, at its roots, with your relationship to your Creator, Higher Power, Power Source, whatever you know exists that controls those things about you that you can not.

By way example, everyone knows that they don't control their bodily functions. We can eat healthy, exercise, get a full eight hours sleep nightly and still get sick and/or die. Obviously, what we do with our bodies can help in sustaining life or shortening it. However, there are simple, absolutely necessary functions that we have no control over.

That is the POWER that illuminates you. *That is what it is necessary* to have a very intimate, personal relationship with. Think of it this way: You need to have a good understanding of how it works so that you can use it when needed. In times of distress and trouble, you have to have a place that you go to help restore peace and order to your affairs or you will never be able to produce anything positive or constructive. The people we know who always have drama going on don't have peace and usually there is no real order to their lives. There is always chaos and confusion.

- *The power greater than you*

So, the power that breathes for us, blinks our eyes, beats our heart, digests our food (or not), is the power you have to establish a relationship with. It exists right within you. The Bible says, in 1 Corinthians 6:19: "What, know ye not, that your body is the temple of the Holy Spirit?"

That spirit, power, abides right in you and you need to know how to access it in this troubled world we live in. Speaking for myself, it is the stabilizing force in my life. Challenges come regularly. I lean on that source for instruction, direction, guidance, intelligence, information gathering (discernment), comfort, companionship, inspiration, joy, happiness and peace. Then, I am careful to show gratitude for the results, even if they are not what I wanted.

I cannot tell you what will work for you, I can only tell you what has worked for me. I listen to that voice inside my head and spirit. I have learned to trust IT over what I see on the outside. When I look outward, often what I see can be misleading. I have simply had better results looking within for the answers and recognizing that if I can find a universal spirit law, immutable principle in Heavenly affairs that supports what I hear in my spirit and mind, I follow it's direction. I found that if it appears to have failed in my eyes, its only because I, somewhere along the way, misunderstood the message.

I believe that we are what we believe we are. We can have what we believe we can have. We cannot, however, have more than we believe we are entitled to or deserve. Non-belief removes the requirement to work hard to achieve. A very smart woman named Angela gave me one of my favorite sayings: "There's no such thing as a free ride in a fancy car."

It is so simple, but so true. Anything worth having is going to require work. Usually, very hard work. Things will not come without challenge. The challenge is not to the effort, but to your belief in yourself and the matter. This is where your faith is tested. Your belief and understanding of your power source is tested here. If you can be deterred from the vision, you will turn back and are not yet ready for the responsibility of the manifestation of the vision.

The practical steps to having the correct relationship with yourself include the following: Examine your self-concept. Ideally, who would you like to be? What are you currently -- what is the reality of who you are right now? Do the two match? If not, and usually they do not totally line up because we are not perfect beings, then there is work left to be done. People have started using a statement that they think is cute: God is still working on me. Yeah, well, He's working on everybody. If he has no further work on us, then we simply wouldn't be here. It is not an excuse to remain as you are. Your self-concept is the foundation of what you believe about yourself. It is the launch pad for every action or non-action.

Prepare a list of self-improvement items. Wherever you find that your ideal version of you is not what you currently are, make a list of areas that need to change to make the ideal match the current version as much as humanly possible. That list is your very first assignment. Make a list of changes you need to make, what *behavior change* looks like and work on that until you have mastered each one you identify.

Remember that there may be things that need to simply be added to your behaviors in order to become the ideal version of yourself. An example might be that you *add to your behaviors* saving $5 per month. When you have improved your self-concept your attitude will greatly improve, your outlook on life and the world of possibilities will be more positive in general. This will attract more positive results and you are now ready to move forward.

Identify your power source, learn how it works, trust it and become dependent on it, rely on it, swear by it, never forsake it. This power source is in all of us. We just don't listen to it. It is that "something" that told you to do or not do something that when you didn't listen to it, it cost you big time. When you did listen to it, it worked out great.

This is not "deep" or out-of-reach for you to understand. Everybody has the same access to *their* power source. I don't have access to yours or anyone else's to the degree that I have access to my own power source. You are what you've been looking for. We should never be looking for the answers to our problems from power sources outside us. These are examples of how I know I am being directed from my power source. They may not be the same indicators for you, but you surely have "tells" just like me because I am no more special than anyone else.

If I have telltale signs that my power source is speaking to me from within (as opposed to me thinking up ideas of my own) then you have yours. Most often I will have an idea or thought that seems to come out of nowhere. It may be intriguing or just interesting. If I do not explore it on that thought alone, then I receive the thought again or someone will discuss the same thing and it confirms exactly what my thought was.

If I still do not acknowledge the thought and begin to take action, I will receive a more urgent push when the thought comes again or some event will happen that makes it necessary for me to move on the original thought. The pressure to act on the thought intensifies each time I do not move.

I like to describe the sequence of thoughts as, to take a term from Oprah, first it comes in the whispers, then waving flags, then flashing lights, then billboards, then 2 x 4's over the head, then run over by cars, buses, trucks or trains and then, which I hope never to get to, an institution. I feel the urgency in my stomach. If something is critical, I often get butterflies. I am explaining my feelings and indicators. You have your own. Find out what system your power source uses in your mind, body and soul to communicate with you. Then trust it with everything you have. You will not be perfect, because we often misread the cues we get from the source, but I have found that I make mistakes less often and the ones that I make are correctable without major damage done. I have also found that there is a blessed protective hedge that exists inside the power source. As long as my intention is to obey, be faithful and loyal to that source, even when I fall short, I am protected. Life is a series of ups and downs. The downs are fewer when I intend to honor and obey my power source.

• *You are what you've been looking for*

Your body is the temple of the Holy Spirit, which is the Comforter that was promised to be sent to those that believed in the Messiah. If your body is the temple, it is where the Holy Spirit lives. Everybody who believes in any higher power is trained to go to that power for solutions to all situations. The only problem is that we tend to think it lives somewhere outside us, above the sky, in our pastor, in our children, in our job, in that fine man about 6'2" -- oh, I digress.

It is critical to realize that you are the answer (solution) to all of your problems and desires. What do I mean? If you don't like the condition of your life, you are the only one who can make the changes. You are the only one who knows the real cause of your problems. Since only the people that created the problem can truly know where to go to destroy the problem, you as an integral part of every situation you find yourself in, have the information necessary to eradicate the problem with the most efficiency and permanency.

Other people can offer advice, wisdom and information, but the best decision will always be the one that comes from within you after careful review of all available information. The key is to trust those decisions. Think of it this way: A recipe for disaster is too many cooks in the kitchen. If you rely too heavily on the input from outside yourself, you are likely inviting too many cooks into your kitchen. If everybody comes into the kitchen and adds "a pinch of salt" to the pot without knowing that the other cooks did the same thing, the likelihood that the dish is going to be too salty gets pretty high.

On the other hand, if the other cooks suggest a pinch of salt and allow the cook to add it, when the last three cooks suggest adding a pinch of salt, the cook can filter that suggestion through all of the other information already available and make the best decision. You are the head chef in your kitchen. The best dish ideas come from the head chef in successful restaurants. Well, the best decisions for your life come from you as the head chef. Put on your hat and cook, baby!!!

In order to be able to determine what information is needed to make the best decision you can make right now, you have to first know yourself. You have to have a definite plan for what you want to see in your situation. *Without a vision, the people perish.* So if you don't have a full understanding -- clear vision -- of your desired outcome, you can't determine if any information you receive is useful.

It is impossible for anyone to give you useful information because you have an undefined outcome. So before you begin to ask for advice or listen to the opinions of others, you have to be sure you can explain to yourself what you really want. Once you have a clear vision of what you want, then you can sort through information or the facts presented, and make the best decision for your situation at that time.

If you don't already know you and what motivates you, that MUST be your very first step to having healthy relationships. The first one has to be a healthy relationship with yourself.

• *Treat myself like a business*

When I was learning how to value myself, it helped me to look at myself as a business. I have been in business for years. There are some principles to running my business that I had to apply to me and my personal relationships. In business, I only have so much time, money and energy to dedicate to any business venture. So I doled out my precious business energy to projects that would benefit the business in some way. It was not just about making money.

Sometimes it was in furtherance of a mission or cause. That was often more important than making money.

When it came to relationships in my personal life, I expended a lot of energy on projects that didn't benefit me. There was very little return on my investment. Even when it came to acquaintances, I might push myself to show up for them but they never showed up for me. I began to understand that spending that energy was a poor business decision for me as the business. If people are not investing in me, then I should not be in relationship with them. Specifically, if a man can't do something as simple as call when he says he will, then he certainly is not making enough of an investment in the Noreen business to receive royalties of my time, energy, money and sex!

And yes, I consider all of those precious. I spent many years working to ensure that I was qualified to be in a relationship. When I finally got myself together, I had to take another step. I had to begin to ask whether the person I was allowing to collect royalties had ever made the necessary investment in me to get the royalties requested.

Like me, they had to have the first relationship -- with them -- in order. Then they had to be able to tell me what it is that they wanted. Why is this important? It is important for me to know what they want so that I can determine whether I am capable of paying that tab, providing that service, delivering that product.

If they can't define what they want, how can I tell if I will be able to fulfill the order? Then I need to evaluate whether they *are* what they are asking to receive. People need to be what they want to receive. The law of attraction dictates this. If you lie to people, people will lie to you. So I began to evaluate if the person walks the talk of what they want to get from me. I met a great guy. He called me when he was going through things. I was a comfort to him. However, he would not always answer my calls. So, in effect, he was not there for me when I needed comfort. He was not, to me, what he allowed me to be to him.

In this particular case, even though he was there for lots of people and that was part of what made him such an amazing person, because he was not there for *me*, it didn't matter how good he was to everyone else.

His *investment* was in *them* and not *me*. Therefore, it would have been an unwise decision for me to allow him to collect the royalties of my time and energy above whatever level I wanted to invest in him. In other words, I only made myself available to be with him as often as I felt comfortable. That way I never felt taken advantage of. I don't have sex with him because he didn't make an investment at that level to get those kinds of royalties.

That brings me to this point. As with any business, there is a menu of services. Even if the menu is very limited, you can't have everything on the menu for a single investment. At a minimum, you have to pay for each item. So, there is a menu of services available in the Noreen business.

In order to partake in any of them, there is a level of investment that everyone needs to make. Even if you are an acquaintance you have to invest something of value. You can't serve no purpose and definitely not be a drain on me and remain a part of my life. Once I began to only pay royalties into relationships that benefited me in some way, the drama was reduced to almost none and I began to have much healthier relationships.

In fact, the Noreen business got pretty good. Suckas need not apply. I must have put a sign on my forehead. Once I began to realize that everyone I meet does not automatically get access to my time just because they come into my life, I have to make a determination about how much access they get to me based on their qualifications. I wouldn't let a dog groomer perform heart surgery on me, no matter how nice, how cute, how friendly or even how efficient and well-trained a dog groomer he or she is. Thus, no matter how nice, cute, friendly or financially stable a man may be, if he doesn't invest in me the things that I need then he can't have access to all of my available services or royalties.

A small investment produces a small return in any business or endeavor. So why should anyone that makes a small investment of time and effort in being involved with me get access to everything that I am: wisdom, advice, fun, intellect, knowledge, sass, wit, sexy, style, grace and so on? Exactly, they shouldn't. The more investment you make, the more services you are eligible for. Make no mistake, sex is the highest level of investment. I don't do well in casual sexual relationships. Either I want more and don't like feeling like a piece of meat or he doesn't like feeling like a piece of meat and ends the situationship.

Remember, the soundest relationship we have to have is the one that starts with the person closest to you -- YOU. It requires spending some time with yourself to find out who and what you are and more importantly what behavior you respond to. For a long time, I appeared to have the self-love and respect necessary to be ready to be in a healthy relationship. In some areas, I did. I knew my place as a woman based on spiritual principles. I am feminine. I have the requisite skills to care for a relationship. Where the behavior was not healthy was in the balance area. I knew better than to give myself totally to a person who was involved with someone else and thus not physically available to me.

However, I did not ensure that the behavior that followed proved that he was emotionally available to me. I was violating balance. Therefore, no matter how I slice it, I was not healthy enough to have the relationship that I knew I deserved.

• *Self-evaluation and self-valuation*

It is critical that we self-evaluate our beliefs and behaviors to understand what behavior we respond to as opposed to what we say we want. This means that we have to take some time with ourselves to be able to identify the unhealthy elements in us. As long as we are looking outward for the answers, we will never find the ultimate answer. People will be happy to offer their opinions on our situations and our character flaws and what it will take to correct the mistakes we have made. But until we look within, where every answer for US is stored, we will hit and miss the target that will stop the pain and hurt.

Self-evaluation takes courage. It requires us to acknowledge our flaws. This is never an easy thing to do. The benefits that result far outweigh any discomfort we feel in the process. The benefits are long lasting. They prevent future hurt and pain. Self-evaluation is where the learning takes place. It is the place that our power source is correcting us in love. He is lacing us with knowledge. We gain perspective and clarity about who we are and what we want. This sets us up to be able to convey that to the people we are in relationship with.

Self-valuation is just that. It is where we place a value on our time, energy, talents and resources. We have to know our worth before we can put a price on it. How can you be a business and not know the value of the services you offer? Even if the business owner charges too much for services, I have never had a business owner tell me they did not know how much they would charge for their services.

Well, it is time to treat yourself as a business in this regard. There is a price, not necessarily monetary, for the privilege of spending time with you, having access to your gifts, talents and time and certainly access to your body, finances and home. You decide that price. That is not a value others should be deciding.

More often than not, if given the opportunity to set a price for anything, the best price everyone knows is free. Being with you should not be free. Nor should you expect to have a great relationship for free. It requires investment to have anything good. Anything worth having is worth working for.

It is true, especially in relationships. We should stop selling ourselves cheap. There should be no fire sale for your time, talents, body and life. All of these are precious gifts given to you by a Creator that He paid for with a great price.

Your body is the house He lives in. If you wouldn't want anyone to do to Him what you are allowing an unhealthy person to do to you, then you should put an end to the behavior. Now. Not later. No, it is not complicated. No, there is nothing here to see. Just stop it. Move on. Wait for the right one.

• *Repair the damage to yourself and heal*

Once we have identified the unhealthy elements in us, we have to repair the damage that we have created or that has been done to us. It may take some time to repair the damage. The first step requires time alone. That is usually the hardest part, especially for people who don't like to be alone or who have abandonment issues.

At first, it will probably feel like you are suffocating, but it will get better and eventually, you will appreciate time alone to enjoy your own company. It is also the place where you have to admit to yourself that you were responsible for a lot of the hurt and pain you suffered based on your unhealthy elements.

There is no other way to accomplish the first part but to do it alone with the help of the Creator inside you. This is an INSIDE JOB. Once that is accomplished, it is vital that you stop allowing those elements to exist in you and your relationships. Practice makes perfect.

I found that once I identified my own mess, I could see the warning flags earlier. I did not always heed them on the first wave, but I would get off the Hurt People Highway a lot sooner. It was like being in school. Once you were taught a subject matter, you were given a test to see if you retained and understood what you learned. This is no different. Yes, you will resolve never to allow another person to hurt you the same way the last one did. And, if you do the work on yourself, no one ever will. That does not mean that no one will try. Someone will test your resolve. Sooner or later, it will fade away of its own nothingness. Each element will cease to exist with you. The interesting thing is that you will be able to identify those elements in others as clear as the nose on their faces. No matter what they *say*, you will know if they will live up to those words or not.

It is interesting that even their choice of words will tell you if they are over it or not. On so many occasions I have listened to people rant and rave about how tired they are of the drama in their relationship and that they are done and I knew they were not done yet. I am not sure if it is simply the words themselves or if it is just the difference in sound between unadulterated truth and wishful chatter, but I can always tell when the person is not really "there" yet.

Do not be discouraged if you meet someone who at first appears to be free from your usual unhealthy elements only to find out later that they have the same elements just in a lesser form or they cover them up better. This will happen for some time because the residue from the old you is still there. It attracted to you, although in a better package with less potency, because the residue or scent remains.

Our unhealthy belief system does not fall away all at once. At some point, it must cease to exist and then the unhealthy person attracted to those elements will no longer be attracted to you. This, again, does not happen all at once so you have to be diligent in calling out the behavior for what it is and respond accordingly. I cannot pacify the emotionally unavailable type. I must recognize it and walk away from it. It is dangerous for me to believe that I can deal with a little bit of emotional unavailability.

That is like saying a substance-addicted person can use that substance once-a-day. Nonsense. A person is a cigarette smoker whether he or she smokes one cigarette per day or two packs. He or she is not qualified as a non-smoker until the smoking ceases.

That does not mean that the urge to smoke completely disappears. That takes time. They will still want that after-meal smoke or to smoke when they have a cocktail because those were the times they enjoyed cigarettes the most. The craving will not immediately disappear, but continued resistance to the urge will cause the cravings to cease over time.

Nobody does everything wrong in a relationship. Even a broken clock is "right" two times a day. Once the unhealthy elements are identified and the damage repaired, what remains should be a healthy you ready for a healthy relationship.

Take the road that leads to these elements. Enjoy the fruits of your labor. Do not sabotage the work you have put in by labeling this potential relationship boring or just not your type. That is exactly what you need. You need to resist the type you have always chosen and open yourself up to a new type. The key is not to put a new face on the old mess and call it fixed, but to actually fix the problem.

I am not suggesting that anyone should be in a relationship with someone that they are not attracted to or are not compatible with. I am offering that what is attractive will change at some level. What was exciting before will no longer be necessary to "feel something" for a new partner. It is perfectly fine not to have that giddy, over-the-top excitement at the beginning of a relationship.

If you want to be in a long-term relationship, it will have to build over time anyway. It will always require spending time with someone before you build the foundation for a long-lasting relationship. This is true because it requires consistent, dependable behavior to be able to truly rely on a person. This builds trust into the foundation of the relationship. To have trust, there will have to be consistent honesty to support placing trust in someone.

This leads to one of the most important elements you must give any relationship -- time to develop. Do not rush into sexual behavior too soon. It clouds our vision and judgment. We miss the small warning signs that this person has the old unhealthy elements that have plagued us before.

Steve Harvey calls it a Ninety-Day-Rule. I am not sure if it is 90 days or not, but I am certain that waiting provides the space to view the person you are interested in objectively. It also allows time for the pretender to show their true colors.

A person can only fake it for so long. Sooner or later, the real is going to come through. If we are high on their sexual drug, we are prone to miss the real, or worse, excuse it and proceed right onto the Hurt People Highway. The goal is to never check into Heartbreak Hotel. These are institutions that result from insisting that the unhealthy is what we must have. We were given free will and if that is our will, the Creator will allow us to have that. He will also allow us to have the consequences of that will. Choose wisely.

• *The order of things*

Another thing we can do to give us a better chance at having a healthy relationship is to play to our strengths. In a world where things appear to be out of control, people want to know how to feel more in control of their basic circumstances. How do I juggle education, work, family, fun, personal interests and keep them all on a healthy track. We want at least some of these elements to go well. When any of these areas of our lives are out of whack, it tends to make us anxious and stressed.

Part of the reason our lives get out of control is because we are out of order. What? Nobody wants to play their natural -- best suited -- position. We all want to play somebody else's position. Everybody wants what they can't have. If I'm short, I want to be tall. If I'm thin I want to be thick. If I'm single I want to be married. Nobody wants the position they're in.

As a result, we have used our free will to bully our way into somebody else's position. We don't recognize that every position is important. No position in anything worth engaging in is a solo activity. Even a sole-proprietor of a business has employees who assist them.

We have to recognize that there IS AN ORDER THAT WORKS BEST. It is the order that lines up with universal law. There are very specific things that the male species is best suited for and things that the female species is best suited for. When parents are parents and not friends, the family functions best. When the man of the house is the father and provider, the household functions best. This is true even if the woman of the house works also. I managed Little League football for years. Our team was very successful. We trained our team that a successful play on offense or defense was simply a matter of everybody playing their position. If the players on the defensive line and the defensive backs all do their job, the other team will not score. But every member has to play their position. If they fail, somebody else has to "step up" and cover that position. That leaves their position open and if the safety can't get in position soon enough to stop the opponent, the other team scores.

In a healthy relationship with a significant other, everybody has to play their position. There are certain roles that have to be fulfilled in every relationship. Let's use the body as a metaphor for a healthy relationship. The body is an amazing piece of

211

machinery that, unless there are ailments or disease, it handles a vast array of functions simultaneously and seamlessly. The body parts, however, do not argue with one another about which part is more important. Each part simply handles the functions it is DESIGNED BY DIVINE ORDER TO HANDLE. Not that a person couldn't pick up a coin with their toes, but it is simply more efficient to use your fingers. The body has one head. Any body that has two heads is considered malformed. The body has one heart. It has two hands and two legs. Each body part works in conjunction with the other parts. If my head itches, one or both of my hands scratch it. The feet don't argue with the hands to "let us" scratch the head. It sounds ridiculous. The feet don't feel a need to "have equality" with the hands to scratch the head. The hands don't accuse the feet of being gold-diggers for not scratching a body part that itches.

When a relationship is healthy, there are lots of functions that are handled simultaneously and seamlessly. The household finances are managed efficiently, the children are nurtured, educated and supported, there is fun and, in general, the members of the family are happy or content. When basic functions are not handled, it creates dis-ease in the relationships and the functions of the family unit.

- *Who is supposed to lead in the relationship?*

Everybody wants to be in charge! Until the bill comes due or the hard decisions need to be made, that is. In the United States, there is a constant struggle for equal rights. It is only fair, according to the United

States Constitution, that everyone in America is treated equally.

However, in divine order, there is no NEED to be "equal" because every part has a relevant function to play. The building block of all matter is the atom. It is so small that it cannot be seen with the naked eye. Yet, it has no need to "be seen" and considered "equal" with any other atom. It is divinely imbued to know that nothing is built without it. Its position in power is established and it is not diminished because another atom is around or combines with other atoms to become a cell. It simply IS and will be combined with the appropriate, effective atoms to form the cell IT WAS DESIGNED TO BE. What the heck does all that mean?

It means that atoms don't have to fight for a right to be equal with anything because they are sure of their place, value and relevance. If you know someone who always has to be seen, at any cost and in the most inappropriate times, it is annoying. They don't usually know that everybody sees them. We hear them. We are painfully aware that they are around. Why? Because they won't just BE, they work super hard to get all of the attention. In order to do this, they have to take attention away from everybody else in the room.

People often say a relationship is a 50/50 proposition. However, if we look at the function of the body, every cell of every organ is important and must play its role in order for the organ to function properly. The cells have no need to be equal with other cells or the organ that it serves. Its power and position have been declared when the cell was just an atom. It has no need to fight the other cells for position. It simply needs to do its job.

However, it must give all of its power and talents in order for the organ and, ultimately, the entire body to function harmoniously. If any cell does not give all for the benefit of the entire body, it is inevitable that the body will be out of sync. Being out of sync has side effects: hurt, pain, disease, suffering and even death. So like the body, a relationship needs every cell in it to give all of its power and talent to the service and function of the relationship. This is not 50/50, but 100/100. There is no need to have the same position or job as the other person because without what you have it is out of sync and the result is hurt, pain, disease and can lead to death if not corrected.

Women have been fighting for equal rights in the United States for decades. It is appropriate that we be paid equal pay for equal work, have the right to vote, make choices over our finances, bodies and circumstances. Where it has created a problem is when we bring that mentality into an intimate relationship. Even if it is a same-sex relationship, one party must assume the leadership role. Just as everybody must have a head. Every relationship must have a head. While women are capable of doing almost anything that men can do, and yes, sometimes better (I digress), it is not the most efficient thing for women to have to do everything. The same is true for men. Men are capable of doing almost anything a woman can do, but it is not always the most efficient way for the benefit of the entire family.

In a family unit, it is most efficient for the head of the household to be the man. I hear all of the screams

Where Do We Go From Here?

and I'm sure I will have to have bodyguard protection from here on out, but it is most efficient. What does that look like? Well, the man should be the provider, protector and leader of the family. Just as the head (the brain) makes decisions for the rest of the body, the man should have the final responsibility for decisions for the family. Now, if he is as efficient as the brain, he will ensure that everyone receives enough power to function efficiently. When that happens, the body is healthy. If the man is efficient in all of the many responsibilities that come along with being the leader, every member of the family will be seen, heard, loved and content.

Now for all of those men out there high-fiving me, think about all of the things you are responsible for. The brain sends and receives messages to every part of the body. That means that it has a connection with every part of the body. If connection is lost with any part of the body, that part of the body becomes paralyzed. When the head of the family fails to maintain a connection with any part of the family, paralysis sets in in the relationship and will affect the entire rest of the family. If the head is not leading and setting the direction for the family, it very likely will not be working as efficiently as it could. Something will be out of order. The head of the family has a lot of responsibility to go along with the authority to make the decisions. He can't have the authority without the responsibility. This is why many women are unwilling, and even afraid, to allow a man to make decisions because many men are not taking and handling their responsibilities.

- *Man created first — HE was given dominion, responsibility for everything, not the female*

When the creation was made, the man was created first. The Creator gave HIM dominion over everything and allowed him to name all of the creatures of the field. The woman came from him. She was not given dominion. The good news is that she was not given the *responsibility* for managing it all. How many times, as a woman, have you felt overwhelmed because there were too many responsibilities on your plate with little or no help?

In the Bible, in the story of creation, it is said, in Genesis 1:26-27:

And God said, Let us make man in our image, after our likeness: and let them have dominion over the fish of the sea and over the fowl of the air and over the cattle and over all the earth, and over every creeping thing that creepeth upon the earth.
So God created man in his own image, in the image of God created he him, male and female created he them.

However, it was not until the next chapter that the woman was drawn out of the man. Genesis 2:18

And the LORD God said, It is not good that the man should be alone; I will make him an help meet for him.

Genesis 2:21-22

*And the LORD God caused a deep sleep to fall upon Adam,
and he slept; and he took one of his ribs, and closed up the
flesh instead thereof;
And the rib, which the LORD God had taken from man,
made he a woman, and brought her unto the man.*

So it is clear that when he created the man and gave him dominion, the woman was not yet brought forth or drawn out of him, so dominion over everything that was created, was given to the man and not the woman. Man was also given the ultimate responsibility for it. Genesis 2:15 says:

*And the LORD God took the man, and put him into the
garden of Eden to dress it and keep it.*

Sounds a lot like responsibility to me.

The order of these events is relevant to us even today. The man is ultimately given dominion along with responsibility. The woman is to be a "help meet for him". The word "meet" has various meanings, but one of those, as an adjective is: ***precisely adapted to a particular situation, need, or circumstance: very proper.*** So Eve was being designed as help precisely adapted to the particular situation, need and circumstance for which she was created.

I have said many times before, that it is NOT a compliment to call me a "strong Black woman." It only reminds me of all of the responsibilities I have had to handle that were not mine. It reminds me of all of the times that men in my life didn't fulfill their role and I had to step up. When no man protected me, I had to protect myself. When no man provided for me,

Where Do We Go From Here?

I had to provide for myself. When no man provided for my son, I had to provide for him. When the men who loved me didn't take responsibility for me, I had to love and take responsibility for myself.

I must say, however, that I have been loved by a long list of men. In fact, I can honestly say that any man that has spent any real time with me loved me then and still does. But as the saying goes, "What's love got to do with it?" Love has a lot to do with a healthy, successful relationship. It's just that it requires other functions, too. Just as the heart in the body, which is a symbol of love world wide, circulates blood and life to the entire body, alone, it is not enough. The brain must send the message to the heart and the rest of the body parts to receive the love and function in order for it all to work efficiently.

In the Bible, the story of Adam and Eve's transgression is well-known. In fact, lots of people blame Eve for all of the suffering in the world. However, if you carefully read the story, you will find that the actual punishment and banishment did not happen when Eve ate the fruit. It happened when "she gave it to her husband and he ate." That was because HE was responsible.

Genesis 3:6-7 reads:

And when the woman saw that the tree was good for food, and that it was pleasant to the eyes, and a tree to be desired to make one wise, she took of the fruit thereof, and did eat and gave also unto her husband with her; and he did eat.

I want to point out the ";" after "with her."

It indicates that while it is a part of the same sentence, the next action is a distinctly separate act. It could stand on its own. It may not seem like a big deal, but it is important. It is a very distinct, stand-alone act that had very real consequences.

Verse 7 continues:

And the eyes of the both were opened and they knew that they were naked; and they sewed fig leaves together, and made themselves aprons.

When we read verse 24, we find that Adam was banished:

So he drove out the man; and he placed at the east of the garden of Eden Cherubims, and a flaming sword which turned every way, to keep the way of the tree of life.

So we read that there was no transgression when Eve alone ate. He drove "the man" out of the garden. Why? Because the man was given the dominion but also the responsibility. So for all of those men who were high-fiving me a little while ago because I said that the man should lead the relationship, it comes with a great amount of responsibility. You cannot have the authority without the responsibility. Man was created and assigned this massive job. In fact, the commandment not to eat was given to Adam before Eve was created from his rib.

Genesis 2:15-17 reads:

And the LORD God took the man, and put him into the garden of Eden to dress it and to keep it.

And the LORD God commanded the man, saying, Of every tree of the garden thou mayest freely eat;

But, of the tree of the knowledge of good and evil, thou shalt not eat of it: for in the day that thou eatest thereof, thou shalt surely die.

Remember, it was not until *after* this in verse 2:21 that Eve was created. But she knew the commandment, because she was within the man when it was given. Going back to Genesis 1:27,

So God created man in his own image, in the image of God created he him, male and female created he them.

So in effect, Eve was there when Adam was created and knew the commandment, but the Creator was very clear who would be responsible. He gave Adam the dominion over and responsibility to name every creature. This was done before he took Adam's rib to create Eve. There was to be no confusion whose responsibility it was to lead. The fact that Eve knew the law when she was approached by the serpent did not mean that she was responsible for it.

I would be remiss not to mention here that all of their behavior was for a purpose. It was planned that the transgression would happen. It was the purpose of the Creator to bring them out of the garden into earthly suffering because he was going to show His power over their transgression and relieve them of the suffering by moving it out of the way in the personage of the Messiah at an appointed time.

- *He will only rise to the level of the woman he is willing to accept responsibility for*

A man will only rise as high as the level of the woman who he is willing to take responsibility for and be responsible to. That does not mean that she controls him. It means that she has been given the ability to inspire him to believe in himself when others doubt him or when he doubts himself. She can build him up and give him the strength to move forward. A major mistake that women make is failing to support the best part of their man because they feel the need to point out all of his flaws and keep his feet planted firmly on the ground.

We see how much influence Eve had. When she influenced her husband to eat, he suffered. Likewise, if she influences him to be his best self, he can achieve great things. Men have a tendency to stay with the woman who does not challenge them or require them to reach higher because it is easier and it doesn't require them to function from their highest self.

The woman who will be a mere convenience for a man and not require anything from him often gets his time, but not his heart and certainly not his last name. Men will use a woman who makes herself available to be used. Period. It is not their fault that we make ourselves available only when they want us.

The unintended consequence for the man, however, is that he is not challenged to get outside of what is easy or convenient. The last time I checked, nobody ever accomplished anything great from a place of convenience or ease. Likewise, as long as a man refuses to step outside of "comfort" to be vulnerable to a real woman with the skills to uplift and support him, he will never reach his greatness.

Some mothers have been able to propel their sons to greatness, but it is a role designed for his wife. There is something extra special about the effects of pillow-talk that make the encouragement and belief more effective in inspiring men to be great.

It may be that men perceive their mother's belief in them as "built-in" or "expected" and not earned. Men feel better when they earn. Whether it is money, attention, respect or affection, men respect and appreciate it if they have earned it. Don't miss that last one, ladies. That is a huge nugget for my female readers. Just so you don't miss it, I will repeat it. Men appreciate and respect affection more when they earn it. I hear Tupac Shakur in my head: "I don't want it if it's that easy. Baby take it easy."

The saying "behind every good man is a good woman" has been passed down from generation to generation for a reason. It's because it's true. A man comes with his own brand of greatness in him. A woman has the ability to influence him to reach for that greatness or influence him to settle for the low-hanging fruit of mediocrity.

Women definitely have the ability to influence a man's decisions. Yes, that started with Eve. Eve influenced Adam to eat the fruit. Even knowing that it was forbidden, her influence was strong enough to get him to go in opposition to what he knew was right. That is strong influence. As I stated earlier, this was for a purpose. There was a reason this was allowed to happen.

However, it does show how strong a woman's influence over a man can be. If women use that influence to encourage, inspire, appreciate and support a man, there are no heights he can't reach. On the other hand, if she uses this influence to cast doubt, point out flaws, discourage change and growth or tear down his self-image, there is no depth he won't sink to, including depression, substance abuse, physical abuse and emotional neglect.

In American society, strength, or the appearance of strength, is valued very highly. We are led to believe that strength is the ultimate power that determines the outcome of all that we want. The truth is love is the most powerful force in the universe. How many stories have we heard of people accomplishing extraordinary things in the name of protecting a loved one? A man next in line for the throne of the British monarchy gave up the throne. Men and women have become estranged from their families to support their choice of spouse. The motivation for all of these actions is love.

Women have been misguided to believe that being equal with a man means that we have to act LIKE men. This is ineffective for most women over the long haul. I have a friend who became involved in a business. One of the female leaders of the business suggested that the women wear suits as opposed to dresses. It was intended to give a "more business-like" impression. What it meant was that it gave a more "masculine" impression. Thus, the underlying theory was that the only way to be business-like is to be masculine in our approach.

My friend, in her infinite wisdom, knew that she did not have to become masculine to be business-like or do good business. In fact, she knew that to remain feminine in her approach to her clients and team was her strong suit and more effective in reaching her goals. Often, women who have been fortunate enough to become leaders in the workforce or business world take the ability to lead into their relationship and it causes conflict with their mate. I have been accused, by men who were insecure in their own position or ability to lead the relationship, of always wanting to be in charge or control. The accusation only came up when I was refusing to go along with or was challenging some behavior on their part and they had no other way to excuse the behavior.

Because I am the boss at work, they assume that I want to be the boss in our relationship. The men who were secure in who they were already could see that outside of my job, I am a woman who wants to be treated like a lady. In fact, in one instance, I had my man ask me why I let him go three or four blocks out of the way and didn't say anything. I reminded him that when I am with him, it is my absolute privilege and pleasure to let him do the thinking. I am grateful to be able to turn that off and let him do the driving and thinking. We had a good laugh about it.

- *Use what YOU got to get what you want (a healthy relationship)*

Women have been socialized to believe that if we lean on our feminine ways to get ahead, we are prostituting ourselves, demeaning our abilities or selling ourselves out. Women who work in the sex-industry are looked down upon. I am not advocating for prostitution, despite it being the oldest profession in the world. Video-cassette makers went out of business, but the sex worker trade has never been out of business. What I am saying is that there is no harm in using our most effective skills and tools to get ahead. In recent times, there have been a lot of stories in the media about men in power taking advantage of that power to sexually harass women and in some instances force them into sexual situations.

This is a disgusting tactic. Until recently, it was not frowned upon by society. It was almost expected. In particular, in Hollywood, it was so prevalent that it had a name -- "the casting couch." Some women were willing to participate to get ahead. Some felt that if they didn't participate that their careers would be stalled. In many instances, they were right. The women who were willing to participate were looked down upon. Tell that to their bank accounts. These women's talents and successes were reduced in the minds of those aware of their participation in the casting couch because it was perceived that the talent wasn't what actually got them where they are.

It was the fact that they were willing to trade sexual favors in exchange for an opportunity. The reality is that their talents outside of the sexual arena may be equally as strong, but because they used their body to accomplish it, it is viewed with contempt and condemnation. I strongly believe that there is a way to use our feminine charms without having sex with a man to gain opportunity. It is not fair or right that women have to use sexual favors to get what they want or should be able to achieve on the merits of their talent.

Nobody ever promised us fair. I am not suggesting that we use sexual favors to get ahead. I am suggesting that using the feminine skills that we have and, that are most effective for us, in business is the best way to be effective.

For example, women have an innate ability to nurture more than one person in a family at a time. In business it transfers to great team-building. It translates to being able to see and understand what each team member needs to be successful in their position. It is not demeaning to utilize this innate ability to make our business successful. I recently heard the CEO of Linked-In discuss his notion that managers should manage "compassionately." This would cause managers to recognize the strengths and weaknesses of their employees and place them in the best position to be successful. Even if that meant firing them from the position they held.

How can it be compassionate to fire somebody? Well, if it is clear that their skills will never meet the expectations of the position, it is compassionate to let them off the hook and set them free to find a position that they are suited for. Sometimes, it is best to move the employee to a different position within the company that better utilizes their skill set.

The CEO is making a conscious effort to learn how to do this. For women, it is a skill that came built-in to our DNA. Why not utilize it? We can make that look easy. Nobody can argue with a manager because they fired someone who was not performing. Just because the manager happens to be female and came to the conclusion faster by leaning on her feminine skill set does not demean the decision.

Let's look at it another way. In sports, the worst thing a coach can do is put a player in a position that their skills are not suited for. It is in the best interest of the team to put each player in the position in which their natural abilities, instincts and desires will work. It ultimately serves the team best.

I love football. It always infuriated me to see a coach come to a new team with a system he wanted to use without regard for the personnel on the team. Don't ask a quarterback who can't throw the mid-range pass to be successful in a system that employs mid-range passing. Alter the system to accommodate the skills of your personnel. That is called coaching. The best coaches adapt to the circumstances. They have to be able to adapt. What good is it to build a system around a single skill set without the ability to adapt it to changing personnel?   In football, it is common for players to be injured. Unless all of your players in a given position have the exact same skill set, which is highly unlikely, your system will fall apart because it will only accommodate one skill set.

In his infinite wisdom, the Creator did not create everyone with the same skill set. We may have some that are similar, but not exactly alike. All quarterbacks should be able to throw the ball. But not all quarterbacks can throw the same pass with the same degree of accuracy. In business and relationships, the goal is to be effective and win. So I ask this question: What is wrong with using what you got to get what you want?

In relationships, the goal is a healthy relationship. Notice, I did not say a good relationship. Why? Because good is subject to opinion. Healthy is not. There is a definition for healthy. Despite anyone's best efforts, even a healthy relationship will experience hard times and have bumps in the road.

For example, when a family member passes away, it causes sadness in those who are still alive. This sadness is experienced and expressed differently in people. No two people's response to death will be experienced or expressed exactly the same. The reason is that no two people had the "exact same relationship" with the person that is deceased. Two children can love a parent very much. However, their relationship with that parent is different for each child because they are two different people.

It amazes me how my mother had the ability to nurture six totally different children. I only had one and it was a challenge to meet all of his varying needs. A healthy relationship can survive challenges because it is built on a solid foundation and has a strong structure. Relating it to the body, it has a good bone structure. Our body can carry around the rest of the body. Even when there is an injury to a part of the body, the bones still support it and don't simply discard that part of the body. It sounds ridiculous to even say that.

So why, when we find ourselves with a hurt or injury in our relationship, do we think to get out of it? Maybe it's because we are led to believe that affairs of the heart are not subject to a pattern or any rules. In some respects, there is validity to this thinking because it involves spiritual elements. Namely love. Love is a spiritual principle that is not limited to the physical realm. However, because ALL things are made by and subject to the Creator, even love and relationships function according to a pattern. There will always be elements that conform to a pattern. An unhealthy, abusive relationship tends to have certain elements as its bone structure. Some of its bones are isolation, intimidation, fear, manipulation, guilt, threats and domination. These bones make up the structure in almost all abusive relationships. All of these elements may not be in every abusive relationship, but these are pretty common.

In contrast, a healthy relationship's bones tend to include trust, communication, respect, support, encouragement, affection, appreciation and others. You get the point. The bones of a healthy relationship give the relationship the best chance of success. This is why the goal is to have a healthy relationship. It is designed with elements or bones that give it the best chance to be successful. I have never met a couple who got married with the intention to get a divorce and ruin each other's lives. I have never been to a wedding where the couple promised to disappoint, hurt, deceive and utterly destroy the life of the person to whom they were getting married and upon having children promised to destroy their lives in the process. Can you imagine what the attendees at *that* wedding would do?

In relationships, men are intrigued by feminine women. I have never met a man who wasn't moved more by a woman being sensitive, sweet and feminine than by her ability to fight and nag to get her way or make a point. It is true that you get more bees with honey than salt or vinegar. I learned, from a book entitled *Fascinating Womanhood,* that men can't resist the softer side of a woman. I also learned that men only fight one way -- to win. It doesn't matter that the opponent is the woman they love. Therefore, if you choose to pick a fight with your man, he will fight to win and wonder why you are surprised or hurt that he went for the jugular vein, your weak spot, to win the fight.

I have had much better success in dealing with men in personal and business relationships when I have used my feminine power. What does that mean? It means there are a few things that work better for females than fighting outright. One is the power of my silence. In fact, my son told me that as a child he knew that as long as I was fussing, he was ok, but when I started talking between gritted teeth and worse yet, got quiet, he knew he better change whatever it was he was doing.

In relationships with two very strong manly men, I found it more effective to make my point and shut up! In both relationships, more often than not the man would either let me have whatever I wanted or would come back to apologize and admit that he was wrong about whatever disagreement we had. So many times in relationships when I tried to debate my point, repeat my position over and over or tried to bargain or shame a man into seeing things my way, it didn't work. Even worse, the men began to distance themselves from me.

Now the relationships with the two men that I used my feminine power skills with ended, but it was my choice to end it because they were not ready to be in a relationship with me. I had long since determined my self-worth and realized that just because a man is interested and truly loves me, does not end the list of qualifications he has to have to be in the "Noreen business."

I strongly encourage women to dress feminine, be sweet and kind to their men, don't debate with them unless it is a crucial, extremely important issue, allow them to be the man they choose to be, don't try to change them, support their dreams and never put them down in front of other people. This is the most harmful behavior. I have witnessed it too many times. I was guilty with my husband. If he angered me in public, I checked him in public. If I had mastered my feminine skills I would have said the things that I needed to say to him privately. It may not have changed the outcome all of the time, but it certainly would have led to me getting my way more often than not.

The lyrics to the song *Family Reunion* by the O'Jays, describes the roles of the father, mother and the offspring. These roles are considered very traditional. I am painfully aware that in today's times, many people do not have the luxury of living these traditional roles. Women are so often forced to take on the roles traditionally thought of as that of a man and, increasingly, men are forced to take on the roles traditionally thought of as that of the woman. As explained previously, a woman can typically do anything that a man do and visa versa. However, there are roles that each is more effective at playing. If our society returns to the traditional roles as much as possible, households will run more efficiently, which means that the people in the household are more healthy physically and mentally. Healthy families make up healthy neighborhoods or communities, which in turn, makes up a healthy society.

There are a lot of mentally unhealthy people walking around. Just because you are not diagnosed as having a mental illness does not mean that you are mentally healthy or mentally stable. I am not a psychiatric professional, but I have to act like one in so many of my life functions. Besides, I know a lot of crazy people. They know who they are, even if they don't readily admit it. But being serious for a second, just because we don't need medication does not mean that everything is all right with us mentally. There are times that we need to seek help to work through trauma, loss, fear and any number of "issues" we face.

Most people shy away from the idea of seeing a therapist. I don't need no therapy! I have heard it so many times from the people that I know need help. They may not be bona fide ill, but if they are not careful and don't address the strain on their mental state, they will become ill. There are circumstances that are so overwhelming that just being able to talk to someone about them helps. Maybe it's just me and maybe it's because I am a woman, but a lot of times just being able to talk through a situation helps ease my anxiety about it. It may not work for you, but it helps me. We can think of it this way: If you don't address a common cold, it can turn into pneumonia. Mental health is no different. If we don't care for our mental state, it can become chronically ill.

- *Why buck the system?*

As we have discussed, there are some systems and approaches that work better than others. The Creator gave males and females certain distinct skills that work best for the roles they were going to have to play. Just as with a football team, why buck the system and try to make a short yardage quarterback into a running quarterback? It just doesn't make sense if the quarterback doesn't have the ability to run very well to put him in a system that requires him to run often. It dramatically reduces the likelihood of success.

Likewise, it is less likely that men are going to be as efficient at the tedious, detailed aspects of running a home as a woman. A woman is less likely to be effective at those things that require upper-body strength. Nobody will fault a woman who does not know how to change a tire. Nor will they fault a man because he does not know how to knit a pair of baby booties.

Why? Because there is a significant amount of strength needed to change a tire. Knitting a pair of baby booties requires nimble fingers and is quite tedious. We never question why we don't fault people

Where Do We Go From Here?

in these positions. In fact, when we hear of a woman accomplishing feats that require great physical strength, we are in awe. When we see a man combing a little girl's hair in a video on social media, it goes viral. That is because we don't expect this from a man.

There is no reason to look down on any couple who chooses to assume traditional roles in a relationship. In fact, the closer to traditional roles a couple can get, I argue, the better their chance of success and effectiveness is.

• *It's all in the selection process*

We often decide that we have sworn off of love. We don't want a relationship. We are tired of being deceived, hurt and taken advantage of. We can avoid this in the early stages -- the selection process. By now, we have cleaned up our own house and are ready to invite in a guest or become a partner with someone that has a clean house. They are healthy and ready to invite someone into their house, too. Our next series of moves will determine whether we have a successful relationship or not. Success is defined by each person or couple.

I will say again that I believe that two consenting adults can consent to whatever they want to consent to. If they achieve what they consented to, whether it is what others think it should be or not, they have a successful relationship. It should not, however, be unhealthy. If it is healthy, it is nobody's business what elements they have chosen. Part of society's problem is always minding someone else's business and not looking at their faults or flaws. We do not have the right to determine what happiness and success looks like for other adults. We don't even get to decide that for our children. Many parents have ruined their relationship with their children trying to force them to be what they want them to be. Because the Creator gave us free-will, everyone resists being forced into any particular lifestyle or behavior. The success of our next relationship will depend in great part on how we select the next partner.

When selecting someone, we have to take into account all of the things we have learned about ourselves. What do we want in this relationship? This may change over time. There have been times in my life when I didn't necessarily want a husband and then there were times when I wanted to be married. In fact, after my Mommy passed away, I knew I wanted a husband. I thought years afterward that it was most likely because she had always been my backbone of support. She was such a larger-than-life super hero to me that I never necessarily felt I needed or wanted a husband. I married young and was aware of all of the work involved so I didn't have a fantasy in my head about what it would be.

I knew I would only marry someone who I felt was worth the effort. It didn't feel like I needed a husband so much until she was gone. In short, because we are humans and alive, our wants, desires and needs are subject to change and grow from time-to-time. In order to select the right person for us at any given time, we have to be honest with ourselves about what we want. We have to know what we want in order to be able to express our needs and wants to another person. One of the biggest mistakes that people make in relationships is assuming that the other person knows, or should already know, what we want and need. This one makes me want to stick a fork in my eyeball. I want to scream: How the hell will they know if you didn't tell them? This assumption is the root of so much misunderstanding, hurt and pain.

Here's what happens. I want or need a certain kind of behavior to feel appreciated and loved. I keep those needs to myself and assume that you already know what they are. You, on the other hand, are expressing your feelings for me through different behavior. You are giving your all in that area and I am still unsatisfied. Sound familiar to anyone? The problem is I never communicated to you what I needed. I probably never communicated it because I haven't done the work with myself to understand what I need and therefore am expecting you to come in and do the work for me.

Just so no one misses this. I need quality time with my partner. He could buy me expensive gifts and not spend time with me and I would be dissatisfied. He would be perplexed as to why his show of affection and interest was not making me happy. Men, as providers, often show their love and affection by providing. They are surprised when women, who often need emotional displays, are not satisfied with them simply working, paying the bills, having a little sex and being left alone. What else does she want from me? He may be willing to provide whatever it is, but if she is unable to tell him what it

236
Where Do We Go From Here?

is, they will argue in circles and resolution will be hard to reach.

It is necessary for everyone to be able to express their expectations for the relationship. This must be done early. Women have to be courageous in asking the question early: What are your intentions toward me? Men have to stop thinking that it means we want to head down the aisle and control you and answer the damn question.

Be honest about your intentions toward us so that we know how much to give. In talking to men, I have found that they know pretty quickly what position a woman can potentially have in their lives. I mean in a few conversations or less. I had a man walk up to me in a club during a NBA All-Star weekend party and tell me that most of the men in that club would never talk to me because when men see me they see responsibility.

He was gorgeous. I was saddened but proud at the same time. I asked him what I could do about it and he said nothing. I had to be prepared to wait for the man who was worthy of me. Coming from him it stung a little but made me proud a lot. For the men out there who see a woman who you perceive will require responsibility and it frightens you, remember that you will only rise to the level of success as the woman who you are willing to be responsible to and for. Translation: If you only want hood-rat quality responsibility, you will always be at hood-rat level in your business and life-style. This is true because the way you approach anything, including having a relationship, is the way you approach everything, including your finances and career choice. Unfulfilled expectations in a relationship of any kind are sure to create dissatisfaction.

Once you have expressed your needs and wants, you have to allow time to see if the person is capable of fulfilling them. This takes time. A person may listen to your conversation and do whatever you said the last person didn't do. They may only be able to do it for a short time if it is not who they truly are.

During this time, you should not be engaging in sexual relations with them. You need to select someone who believes you are worth the wait and that does not think they can gain influence over you through their sexual prowess. You have to be able to view their behavior objectively. You need to be able to see if they are consistent in their behavior.

If they are able to meet your needs and wants and have shown that they listened to your expectations and have met them, you are halfway there. The next thing to be sure of is that you are qualified to do the same for them. You have to be able to meet their needs and wants, and be consistent in meeting their expectations.

This is a two-way street. I know that I am not a good fit for a person who likes to go camping and fishing and being out in the wild. My idea of roughing-it is a hotel with no room service. I would be miserable with an outdoorsman. He would be miserable with me. It does not make either of us a bad person. It just means that we are not compatible. These are the things that we need to explore in the selection process.

Other things we need to look for in the selection process are how people handle their finances. Yes, you should determine, if you are looking for a long-term fit, how this person handles his or her business. Money is one of the leading causes of disagreement in relationships. Do not avoid this conversation if you want to be in a long-term relationship. Before you share housing and financial responsibilities with someone, you need to pay close attention to how they handle their finances.

A person who handles his or her finances poorly will not suddenly become a financial wizard just because you are in a relationship. I know couples who have been together for years living in a weekly motel with only a hot plate to cook on. It works for them. It would never work for me. This is also a choice to be made between two consenting adults. It is not for me to judge. It is also not for me to subsidize either. If you choose to be with a person and your finances are not stable, do not expect others to subsidize your choice. Let me step on some more toes before I conclude.

Anyone who has an adult partner should never ask friends and family to provide basic food, clothing and shelter. If you have ever been put in this position, either asking or being asked, you know this is not a good situation to be in. Grown men and women who handle their financial business are willing to help a single person struggling, but once you add another person to the mix, the dynamics change. I can tell you why that is for me. If I made choices that allow me to be stable financially, I don't believe I should be financially supporting a grown woman who has a grown man.

They are responsible for each other. I am not, after all, reaping the benefits of either person's time, talents or body. What exactly should I be paying for? So if you find that people don't want to loan you money and you have a partner, that might be why. No one can judge you for your choices, but they are not required to subsidize them either. I pay careful attention to how a man handles conflict and the amount of conflict that surrounds him during the selection process. People who are always in conflict are usually the source of some, if not all, of it. The one constant in the drama is them. Whether they know it or not, they are attracting what they are. I pay attention to his response to adversity. These things will tell me how he will handle me during times of conflict and adversity. I need to know if that is compatible with how I need to be treated.

I was in a relationship with a man and his business began to suffer. That would not have been a problem except that he would not speak to me for months. Once the business stabilized he wanted to marry me. I declined because I knew that even if we were married, he would withdraw into himself when things got tough. In my mind, those would be the times that we needed to come together, not retreat into our own shells. I could not live like that. I needed a man who would be my partner in tough times. This man showed me in a crisis that had nothing to do with me how he handled crisis and who he was in crisis. I chose to believe him the first time.

Learn as much as you can about the family interaction of the person you are interested in. It will tell you a lot about how they will treat you in relationship. Childhood and immediate family is where we develop a lot of our behavior in relationships. The more you get to see people interact with their families, or not interact, the more insight you will have into their behavior patterns. You will gain a lot of knowledge without having to ask a lot of questions.

At the end of the day, it all comes down to giving yourself enough time to get to know who it is that you will be in relationship with. If you only want a short-term casual relationship, you may not need to know that much information. You may only need to know what their favorite position is. I don't know. The needs, wants and expectations are purely yours. You may need to know a lot more information because you want a longer-term relationship. Whatever you decide, you have to be honest with yourself and the person that you want it from.

Even if it is only a casual sexual relationship, you have to be honest about that. Sometimes men have pretended they wanted a long-term relationship just to get sex and moved on after they got the sex. I taught my son early in his life that he never has to lie to a woman about that. Women like sex, too. Sometimes, we are willing to have sex with you because we want you sexually. You don't have to lie to kick it. If she is willing, she will do it. If not, there is someone who will.

Even if she doesn't like your truth, she will respect you for speaking it and living it. She will also not feel taken advantage of and get her feelings hurt. If they are, she will have to admit that you were honest from the beginning. That becomes a "her issue" and not a "you issue." She will have to own her choice. We have to allow enough life to happen between us before we can determine if this is a long-term relationship. Taking the time to learn these things before engaging in sexual behavior gives you the clarity and objectivity to see the potential for the relationship for what it is. Do the work in the selection process and save yourself from getting on that crowded Highway of hurt people that leads to hurt people.

Contact the Author
Noreen McClendon
P.O. Box 30316
Los Angeles, CA. 90030
hphighway@yahoo.com

www.ingramcontent.com/pod-product-compliance
Lightning Source LLC
Chambersburg PA
CBHW051820090426
42736CB00011B/1568